Pinch OF Nom
AIR FRYER

Pinch of Nom
AIR FRYER

EASY, SLIMMING MEALS

bluebird

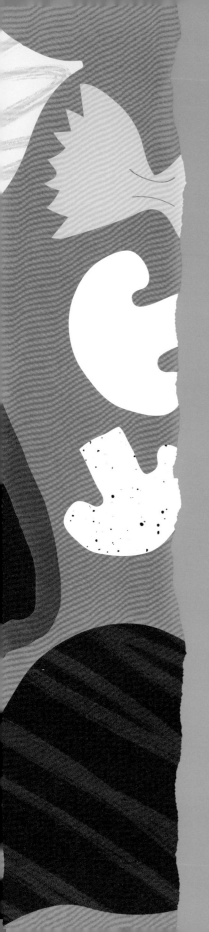

CONTENTS

HELLO

Welcome to our most-requested cookbook ever!

You've been asking us to put together a collection of air fryer recipes for ages and we're over the moon that the day has finally arrived! This cookbook means a lot to all of us at Nom HQ, and we knew it wasn't something we should rush. No matter what kind of air fryer you have at home, or how often you've used it, you can treat this cookbook as a one-stop shop for absolutely everything you need to know. By dreaming up brand-new air fryer dishes and hand-picking tasty classics to adapt, we've made mealtimes quick, simple AND crispy . . . with a slimming-friendly twist!

WHY AIR FRYER?

This cookbook is an exciting new chapter for us because all the recipes are made with one beloved kitchen gadget in mind: your air fryer. We want everyone to enjoy the tasty food in this book, from beginners through to air-frying experts, so we've made sure the recipes are as easy to follow as possible. Air frying is changing the way all of us cook, but we've not changed anything about how we organise things! You can flick straight to the dishes you're in the mood for,

with clearly marked sections for Breakfasts, Fakeaways, Light Bites, Bakes and Roasts and Sweet Treats.

While fried food might not scream 'slimming friendly', air fryers work their magic to give the ultimate crunch with little or no oil needed. This makes them the ideal gadget for rustling up lower-calorie creations that don't compromise on texture or flavour. Not a day goes by where we don't use ours, which is how we've learned a heck of a lot about air frying! We've jam-packed this whole book with handy hints, tips and knowledge to share with you – including an easy-to-follow air fryer to oven conversion chart on page 33.

We like to say you can cook almost anything in an air fryer and honestly, one of our biggest challenges with this book has been choosing what to include! We've focused on packing your midweek menu with flavourful, low-fuss crowd-pleasers that never get boring, like our BBQ Meatloaf (page 122). From making a juicy Whole Chicken (page 106) to crisping up a batch of fluffy-in-the-middle Roast Potatoes (page 126), you can rest assured

that we've got the basics covered too. You'll definitely want to turn to the pages with sweet treats you've not tried in an air fryer before, like our gorgeous berry-topped Pavlovas (page 182).

You know that we love to outdo your local takeaway with fakeaways, and our Salt and Pepper Chips on page 70 prove it. We're also counting on eagle-eyed Nom fans to spot the website favourites that we've transformed into air fryer wonders (Chicken Kyiv Pasta Bake on page 114 is worth bookmarking right now!).

We're absolutely buzzing for you to dig in! We had a whole lot of fun 'shaking up' signature Nom flavours by cooking them in a new way, and we hope we can bring some of that joy to your kitchen too.

Thank you so much for being the best community ever. You've waited long enough . . . ready, set, fry!

Kay Kate
x

ABOUT AIR FRYERS

Like everyone else, we've been blown away by how popular air fryers have become over the last few years. At first, we weren't sure if they'd be just another expensive gadget that quickly went out of fashion, but they've turned out to be a handy bit of kit that lots of us can't live without!

When we decided to create this book, we promised we'd make sure every recipe worked in every different air fryer. Before you start cooking up an air-fried feast, here are a few things you'll need to know.

HOW DO AIR FRYERS WORK?

Air fryers work by circulating a powerful blast of hot air around the basket or drawer. This cooks food really quickly, locking in flavour and making everything mouthwateringly crispy! They'll give you a really satisfying, deep-fried crunch, without the need for lots of high-calorie oil or cooking fat – which is what makes them perfect for slimming-friendly cooking.

Often, cooking something in your air fryer can save you from having to turn on your oven at all. Since air fryers are much smaller than traditional ovens, they're also more energy efficient to use. Although they can be a bit of an investment, if you regularly use your air fryer, it might well save a few pennies on your energy bills in the long run.

It doesn't matter if you have a traditional air fryer or a halogen air fryer; both versions will work for the recipes in this book. There are also a few air fryer models out there that come with a paddle to stir food while it cooks – in general, this can just be removed, but check your product manual if you're not sure.

WHICH AIR FRYER DID WE USE?

To develop the recipes for this book, we used a Dual Zone Air Fryer with a 9.5 litre capacity and 2470W of power.

Don't panic if the air fryer we've used sounds totally different to the one you've got waiting on your kitchen counter! Read on for more information on the differences between air fryer types and how to adjust cooking times to suit yours.

DOES THE WATTAGE OF YOUR AIR FRYER MATTER?

It's well worth making a note of how the wattage of your air fryer compares to the one that we used, as this does have a slight impact on how quickly food cooks. You can find this out by looking for the wattage on the product label, in the booklet that came with your air fryer, or on the manufacturer's website.

Typically, most air fryers will fall between 1200W and 3000W of power. Smaller air fryers will usually have lower wattages, whereas large capacity models tend to need a bit more power. The wattage of your air fryer makes the biggest difference when you first pop your food in the basket. When you add cold food into a preheated air fryer (or oven) the internal temperature will drop a few degrees. Since a more powerful appliance heats up more quickly, it'll climb back up to the desired temperature in less time than a lower wattage model. This is why food will cook a little bit faster in a higher wattage air fryer.

Once you've checked how your air fryer compares to the one we've used, you'll be able to use the cooking times on our recipes as a guideline.

If your air fryer is more powerful, you may need to cook the dishes for a little less time, and if it's less powerful, cook for a little longer. The good thing about air fryers is that it's almost always okay to open the drawer/lid to check on your food as it cooks (any exceptions are clearly flagged in our recipes!). This means you can keep a close eye on your meal, and tweak the cooking time as required to get perfect results.

FUNCTIONS, TEMPERATURES AND PREHEAT SETTINGS

For the recipes in this book, we'll tell you what temperature to set your air fryer to, and how long to cook it for. If your air fryer offers a choice of cooking functions, select the general 'air-fry' setting.

Some air fryers don't allow you to manually adjust the cooking temperature; in this case, check your product manual to find out the temperature settings of each pre-programmed cooking function. From there, you'll be able to select the best match for the recipe you're making.

Lots of air fryers come with a preheat function, and will beep to tell you it's time to add in the food. However, we know that some models don't have a preheat function, so if yours doesn't, just set it to the required temperature and let it heat up for a few minutes before popping the food inside.

DIFFERENT BASKETS, DRAWERS AND SHELVES

Between baskets, dual drawers, grill shelves and paddles, we've seen it all while we were putting this book together! There's always a way to make a recipe work with the air fryer you've got.

Some of the dishes in this book are air-fried straight into the drawer, while others may tell you to use a small ovenproof dish or ramekin. We found that air fryer accessories such as silicone or disposable liners came in handy time and time again when we needed to adapt a recipe. You'll find more details of any bits and bobs that we recommend in Our Favourite Kit on page 24.

AIR FRYER CLEANING AND CARE

It can't be avoided . . . your air fryer has to be cleaned between each use! To keep you safe, any buildup of grease or food crumbs needs to be fully removed before you start cooking. Check if any parts can be placed in the dishwasher, otherwise you should find that removable drawers and baskets are easy to wash by hand. Silicone or disposable liners are really useful if you want to make cleaning even easier.

We've dropped a handy step by step video on how to clean your air fryer, along with lots of other resources, on our website. Use the camera app on your phone to scan the QR code to access air fryer accessory recommendations, buying guides and more. Or, you can go directly to pinchofnom.com/how-to-use-an-air-fryer.

THE FOOD

As a classically trained chef, Kate has always loved recreating dishes and putting an original spin on classic recipes. This is how the very first Pinch of Nom recipes came to be, and it's this passion that means we can continue to bring fresh new flavours to you today. Kate and her small team of trusted recipe developers love nothing more than getting into the kitchen and experimenting with ingredients until some Pinch of Nom magic is created!

It's always been our mission as a recipe team to make it easy to cook healthy, homemade food, and this book is no exception. It's been an exciting learning curve for us to work with just one kitchen gadget, and there's been lots of trial, error and taste-testing along the way! We've taken things one ingredient at a time to find the best ways to adapt familiar favourites, and create totally new recipes. We hope that you'll be able to tell just how much fun we've had experimenting with cooking trademark Nom flavours, in a newer, speedier, crispier way!

To save on time and money, we've kept everything as stripped back as possible, and we've relied on fuss-free ingredients that you can use across multiple dishes. From time to time, you might find a less common ingredient that adds something really special to a dish, but we'll always try to make sure you get to use it again somewhere else.

If you've followed Pinch of Nom since day one, you'll know that it's hugely important to us that absolutely anyone can pick up our books and give cooking a go. All of the recipes we've picked suit any level of cooking skill, so even if you've never used an air fryer before, you'll have no trouble with our slimming-friendly breakfasts, lunches, dinners, sides and desserts.

We've tried to make using this cookbook just as quick and convenient as air-frying itself, by clearly flagging all of our vegetarian and vegan dishes, and adding notes where ingredient swaps can be made. You'll also spot that we've dropped hints and tips around every corner!

RECIPE TAGS

EVERYDAY LIGHT

These recipes can be used freely throughout the week. All the meals, including accompaniments, are under 400 calories. Or, in the case of light bites and sweet treats, under 200 calories. Of course, if you're counting calories, you still need to keep an eye on the values, but these recipes should help you stay under your allowance.

WEEKLY INDULGENCE

These recipes are still low in calories at between 400 and 500 calories, or 200–300 for light bites and sweet treats, but should be saved for once or twice a week. Mix them into your Everyday Light recipes for variety.

SPECIAL OCCASION

These recipes are often lower in calories than their full-fat counterparts, but they need to be saved for a special occasion. This tag indicates any main meals that are over 500 calories, or over 300 for light bites and sweet treats.

KCAL *and* CARB VALUES

All of our recipes have been worked out as complete meals, using standardised portion sizes for any accompaniments, as advised by the British Nutrition Foundation. Carb values are included for those who need to measure their intake.

GLUTEN-FREE RECIPES

We have marked gluten-free recipes with a 'GF' icon. All these recipes are either free of gluten or we have suggested gluten-free ingredient swaps of common ingredients, such as stock cubes and Worcestershire sauce. Please check labelling to ensure the product you buy is gluten-free.

FREEZABLE RECIPES

Look out for the 'Freezable' icon to indicate freezer-friendly dishes. The icon applies to the main dish only, not the suggested accompaniments.

STANDARD FREEZING *and* REHEATING GUIDELINES

For most recipes, you'll be able to follow our standard freezing and reheating guidelines below (we'll let you know if a recipe requires more specific instructions):

· Allow food to cool and then freeze as soon as it is cold enough.
· Place in a container or bag that is suitable for freezing.
· Add a label telling you the name of the recipe and the date you're freezing it

The general consensus is that you can keep food frozen for around 6 months, although after 3 it'll start to lose its flavour.

You should reheat and eat defrosted food within 24 hours. Please don't reheat frozen food until it has defrosted thoroughly in a fridge or microwave. NHS guidelines (correct at the time of writing) state that you should reheat food until it reaches 75°C/167°F and holds that temperature for 2 minutes. Always make sure it's piping hot throughout (you should stir while reheating to ensure this).

Keep cooked rice in the fridge no longer than 1 day before reheating it, or you can freeze it and defrost thoroughly in the fridge before reheating. Always make sure you reheat rice until it is piping hot, and never reheat it more than once.

If you're ever unsure about freezing and reheating a recipe safely, we'd strongly advise referring to the official NHS guidelines.

All of these calculations and dietary indicators are for guidance only and are not to be taken as complete fact without checking ingredients and product labelling yourself.

KEY INGREDIENTS

PROTEIN

Lean meats are a great source of protein, providing essential nutrients and keeping you feeling full between meals. In all cases where meat is used in this book, we'd recommend using the leanest possible cuts and trimming off all visible fat. In many of our recipes you'll find that you can switch the type of protein for whatever meat you prefer. This especially applies to any mince recipes; turkey, beef or pork mince are easily interchangeable – just be mindful that you may need to adjust air-frying times to suit! Fish is also a great source of protein, and it's naturally low in fat. Fish provides nutrients that the body struggles to produce naturally, making it perfect for lots of our super-slimming recipes. And don't forget, vegetarian protein options can always be used instead of meat in all of the recipes in this book.

HERBS *and* SPICES

We love a bit of spice! One of the best ways to keep your food interesting when changing ingredients for lower fat/sugar/calorie versions is to season it well with herbs and spices. Mixed spice blends, either shop-bought or homemade, are great for adding flavour in a pinch. Don't be shy with spices – not all of them burn your mouth off! We've added a spice-level icon to the recipes in this book, so you know what to expect. The beauty of cooking dishes yourself is you can always adjust the heat to your liking – add more or less chilli to suit. Always taste your food before adding extra spicing; spices, vinegars, mustard and hot sauces should be added gradually, to taste.

STOCKS, SAUCE *and* THICKENERS

When you remove fat from a dish, flavours can dwindle. Adding spices is one way to boost flavours, but often the level of acidity in a recipe is much more important. When it comes to balancing and boosting flavours in our dishes, we love to use vinegar, soy sauce, fish sauce, Worcestershire sauce or Henderson's relish. One of Pinch of Nom's essential ingredients is the humble stock cube or stock pot; they add instant flavour and they're so versatile. We use various flavoured stock cubes and pots throughout this book, but there's always an option if you can't get your hands on the exact ones we've used. It's worth noting that sauces, stock cubes and pots are often high in salt, so you may want to swap for reduced-salt versions.

Reduced-sugar ketchup isn't just great for topping chips, it also adds a rich depth of flavour to soups, stews or pasta sauces. You'll want to try a dollop with plenty of the baked-until-golden goodies in this book, including our crispy-coated Potato Dogs on page 154.

From breakfasts to fakeaways and midweek dinners, we often use either syrup or honey to give dishes a touch of sweetness, without drying them out (like the sticky glaze on our Maple-Glazed Gammon on page 128).

We're often asked for tips on how to thicken soups, sauces and gravies. In the pre-slimming days, we wouldn't have thought twice about using a few tablespoons of flour to thicken liquids. Nowadays we're always on the lookout for lower-calorie and gluten-free options. Letting liquids reduce is a good way of thickening sauces without adding anything extra. As the moisture evaporates, the flavours get more concentrated too, so the end result will taste even better.

REDUCED-FAT DAIRY

Substituting high-fat dairy products with clever alternatives can make a dish instantly lower in calories. You'll find that we'll often use reduced-fat cream cheese or spreadable cheese rather than the higher-fat versions.

TINS

Don't be afraid to bulk-buy tinned essentials! Beans, tomatoes and sweetcorn all come in handy time and time again. Using tinned ingredients can really help to keep costs down, and you'll never know the difference.

FROZEN FRUIT and VEG

Frozen fruit and veg make great filler ingredients and are perfect low-cost alternatives anywhere that fresh ingredients aren't always necessary. Most of the time they're already peeled and chopped too, so they save time as well as money; you can just throw them in alongside your other ingredients.

PULSES, RICE and BEANS

High in both protein and fibre, keeping a few tins of beans and pulses in the cupboard is never going to do any harm! Rice is a fantastic filler and a great accompaniment to so many Pinch of Nom recipes.

BREAD, WRAPS and PASTRY

A great source of fibre, wholemeal bread is filling and versatile too. You'll definitely want to whizz up homemade breadcrumb mixtures, as air fryers are brilliant at recreating crunchy deep-fried textures, for a fraction of the calories. We often use gluten-free breads as they tend to contain fewer calories and less sugar, so they're an easy swap when you want to shave off a few calories. Since they're a time-saving alternative to blitzing your own (and available gluten-free!), we've used panko breadcrumbs for our Gochujang Chicken Nuggets on page 80.

POTATOES

It wouldn't be right to talk about air-frying without mentioning the humble potato. No matter what variety you prefer, one thing's for sure: your air fryer will crisp it to perfection. From Sweet Potato Katsu (page 64) to Fluffy Jacket Potatoes with Spicy Tuna (page 138), plenty of our recipes prove you can never have too many spuds on standby. Chopped, sliced, mashed or filled, the 'beep' will tell you when this versatile root veg is fluffy in the middle and ready to serve as a light lunch or side dish.

EGGS

Eggs are protein-rich, tasty and versatile! A simple egg can be used in so many different ways. From baking and binding ingredients together, to having a starring role in our Sausage and Egg Muffins (page 44) you'll never go wrong if you have a box of eggs in the house.

LOW-CALORIE COOKING SPRAY

One of the best ways to cut down on cooking with oils and fats is to use a low-calorie cooking spray. A spritz of this will make little difference to the end result of your food, but it can make a huge difference to the calories consumed.

SWEETENER

There are so many sweeteners out there, it can be tricky to know which is the best substitute for regular sugar. Sweeteners vary in sweetness and swapping them weight-for-weight with regular sugar can give you different results. In our recipes we use granulated sweetener, not powdered sweetener, as it has larger 'crystals'. This can be used weight-for-weight anywhere that you're replacing sugar.

DRIED PASTA *and* NOODLES

We wouldn't want to live without pasta or noodles! They're not too pricey to stock up on, and they'll keep nicely in the store cupboard until you're ready to transform them into fakeaway favourites and midweek classics, like our humble Sausage Pasta Bake (page 110).

SELF-RAISING FLOUR, BAKING POWDER *and* ROLLED OATS

Whether you're an expert or beginner baker, you'll want to make sure you've got self-raising flour. It's an essential ingredient to guarantee the fluffiness of cakes, muffins and other baked goodies. Sift flour together with baking powder to air-fry spongey treats like our White Chocolate and Blueberry Muffins on page 178, until they're risen and golden.

Rolled oats are cracking to have in the cupboard for batch-cookable breakfasts like our Peach Melba Baked Oats (page 50). They're rich in filling fibre that'll fuel you up for the day ahead, or they're just as handy for whipping up sweet snacks and desserts.

OUR FAVOURITE KIT

AIR FRYER

It might seem silly to say it, but you'll need an air fryer to make the recipes in this book (although you can convert the cooking times to work in an oven using the chart on page 33). If you're buying your first air fryer, or in the market for a new one, there are so many different models to choose from. Our advice is to pick an air fryer that best suits how many people you're cooking for, and how often you think you'll use it. Choose a larger capacity if you're cooking for a big family, or look for a model with dual drawers if you want to cook your main and sides at the same time. The main thing to remember is that there's always a way to make the recipes in these pages work, even if your air fryer is a completely different size and shape to someone else's.

AIR FRYER ACCESSORIES

Most air fryers come with all the essential bits of equipment you need to get started. In this section, we've noted down the 'nice to haves' we like to use with our air fryer, but you don't have to buy them all. For even more recommendations and useful resources, scan the QR code on page 12 to visit our online air fryer guide.

TONGS *and* GLOVES

Unlike an oven, it's okay to open your air fryer drawer or lid to check on your food during cooking. You'll want to protect yourself by wearing heat-resistant gloves to give your air fryer basket a good shake, or by using tongs to safely toss, flip and stir ingredients.

BAKEWARE

Air fryers normally come with bakeware bits like racks, trays and baskets. The best ones for you to buy will depend on the size and shape of your air fryer, so be sure to take note of your air fryer's measurements before shopping around. With a baking tray, baking tin or shallow dish, you'll be able to air-fry lots of our recipes. As always, you want to look out for the ones with a non-stick coating – they'll be nice and easy to clean! For rustling up bakery-inspired goodies that are even in size, it's well worth picking up a silicone muffin mould, or you can buy individual muffin cases if you have a smaller air fryer. For making larger showstoppers like our Orange and Lemon Cake on page 186, you'll want to pick up a 25.5x13.5cm loaf tin (we'll always specify if the size of equipment is essential to the success of a recipe, and you'll spot the details listed as 'Special Equipment').

GRILL RACKS *and* SKEWER RACKS

Grill racks and skewer racks are a really nifty cooking tool if you want to take your air fryer to the next level, especially if you'll be cooking meat. Racks are designed to elevate ingredients like mouthwatering steaks, crispy-coated chicken burgers or marinated fish, so that they're exposed to hot air from all angles. This is especially good news if you're looking to achieve a gloriously golden crispy coating! Ingredients that are sliced into chunks can be threaded onto skewer racks; you should be able to turn your kebab-style creations during cooking, to make sure everything's nice and evenly grilled.

BASTING BRUSH

A basting brush will always come in handy for preparing meat, fish or anything where you don't want the item to dry out. Carefully brush your ingredients to make sure they're fully coated, and the flavouring from your sauce, seasoning or spice mix will be nice and evenly distributed. We'll specify where we've used ours throughout the book.

SILICONE LINERS/PAPER LINERS

Liners are an affordable bit of kit that'll help you keep your air fryer in tip top condition, by catching any excess grease while you're cooking. You can buy parchment liners to throw away after each use, but we prefer to wash and reuse silicone liners. They have a much higher temperature resistance than paper versions and they make the clean-up of oily residue even easier!

RAMEKINS

From lava cakes and soufflés to miniature quiches, there are lots of ways you can get creative with ramekins. They're ideal for keeping ingredients tidy that might otherwise cause a bit of a mess inside of your air fryer, like eggs. Crack a couple into a small dish and they'll bake until they're just right for you, with a soft or hard centre.

MEAT THERMOMETER

Some models of air fryer come with a built-in meat thermometer that'll automatically stop cooking when your food has reached the desired temperature. If your air fryer doesn't have this, you can always use your own meat thermometer to help you double-check the temperature of your food. Always insert at a slight angle through a chunky part of the meat for the most accurate measure!

KITCHEN BASICS

NON-STICK PANS

Even for a cookbook that's mostly air fryer recipes, you'll find yourself reaching for a saucepan now and again, to make sides, sauces and other bits on the hob. The better the non-stick quality of your pans, the fewer cooking oils and fats you'll need to use in order to stop food sticking and burning. Keep your pans in good health by cleaning them properly and gently with soapy water. We recommend picking up a good set of saucepans, a small and a large frying pan.

KITCHEN KNIVES *and* KNIFE SHARPENER

Every kitchen needs a good set of knives. If you can, splurge on some good quality, super-sharp knives – blunt knives have a habit of bouncing off ingredients, which can make them more dangerous than sharper ones. You'll need to mind your fingers with super-sharp knives too, but you'll be glad you invested when you've got knives that glide through veg, saving you so much time and effort. Keep them nice and sharp so you can carry on slicing and dicing like a pro.

CHOPPING BOARDS

As well as protecting your surfaces, a good set of chopping boards are the key to a safe and hygienic kitchen. We'd suggest picking up a full set of colour-coordinated chopping boards, with separate boards for veg, meat, fish and dairy. They'll make it so much easier to keep your ingredients separate, and most sets are easy to clean and tidy away once the meal prep is sorted.

FOOD PROCESSOR, BLENDER, STICK BLENDER *and* ELECTRIC WHISK

These are essential pieces of kit for a lot of Pinch of Nom recipes. We like to make sauces from scratch, so a decent blender or food processor is a lifesaver. A stick blender can be used on most occasions if you're looking for something cheaper or more compact. It's well worth the investment for the flavour of all those homemade sauces. An electric whisk is nice to have when you need to whip up a scrummy sweet treat in a hurry.

HOB

We cook on an induction hob from time to time when we're sautéing sauces or other bits of prep that aren't air-fryer friendly. If you have a ceramic/hot-plate hob you may have to cook dishes for a little longer.

MIXING BOWLS

A couple of mixing bowls will always come in handy. We'd suggest getting at least two, a smaller one and a large one will see you through most kinds of recipes. Smaller bowls give you more control when you're whisking ingredients and larger bowls mean more room to mix it up.

PASTRY CUTTERS *and* COOLING RACK

All of your baked goodies will cool down quicker on a wire cooling rack. While it can be tough to resist, resting time is essential to prevent a soggy bottom. For recipes like our Cream Tea Scones (page 190), a pastry cutter will give you perfectly even scone shapes every time.

MEASURING SPOONS

Want to make sure you never get muddled between a tsp and tbsp? Pinch of Nom has absolutely, definitely never made this mistake. Honest. But these days we're never without a trusty set of measuring spoons, which help make sure it's not a tablespoon of chilli when it should have been a teaspoon. Just make sure you use a butter knife to level off the spoon – you'll be surprised how much extra you add when the spoonful is heaped.

HEATPROOF JUG

A measuring jug is essential for measuring out wet ingredients. We recommend getting a heatproof version that you can stick in the microwave when needed.

FINE GRATER

You won't believe the difference between grating cheese with a fine grater versus a standard one. 45g cheese, for example, can easily cover an oven dish when using a fine grater. You can also use it for citrus zest, garlic and ginger – it helps a little go a long, long way.

GARLIC CRUSHER

You'll never miss the faff of finely chopping garlic once you've invested in a garlic crusher. Relatively cheap to pick up, you won't go back after you've squeezed that first clove into a perfect paste. It'll save you so much time and it helps your garlic spread evenly throughout the dish.

WOODEN *or* METAL SKEWERS

Threading meat, fish or vegetables onto skewers means they'll leave the air fryer with so much more deliciously juicy flavour. You can keep turning them for even cooking, and you can make sure every inch of your meat is covered with marinade. Be sure to soak wooden skewers in water, so that they don't catch and burn.

TUPPERWARE *and* PLASTIC TUBS

Many of the Pinch of Nom recipes in this book are freezable and ideal to enjoy all over again as tasty, slimming-friendly leftovers. It's a good idea to invest in some freezer-proof tubs – and they don't have to be plastic. For a more eco-friendly solution, choose glass storage containers; just remember to check they're freezer-safe.

*Note on plastic: We have made a conscious effort to reduce the amount of non-reusable plastic such as cling film when making our recipes. There are great alternatives to cling film now available, such as silicone stretch lids, beeswax food covers, fabric food covers and biodegradable food and freezer bags.

CONVERSION CHARTS

You'll notice there are no alternate cooking methods included in this book, but that's not to say you can't make most of these recipes in an oven if you prefer. In general, cooking in an oven will give results that are just as delicious, although it will take a bit longer and may be a little less crispy.

To help you convert the recipes to oven, here's a handy conversion guide:

HOW TO CONVERT RECIPES TO AN AIR FRYER

OVEN MINS	AIR FRYER MINS
10 MINS	8 MINS
15 MINS	12 MINS
20 MINS	16 MINS
25 MINS	20 MINS
30 MINS	24 MINS
35 MINS	28 MINS
40 MINS	32 MINS
45 MINS	36 MINS
50 MINS	40 MINS
55 MINS	44 MINS
1 HOUR	48 MINS

OVEN	OVEN (FAN)	AIR FRYER
190°C	170°C	150°C
200°C	190°C	160°C
210°C	190°C	170°C
220°C	200°C	180°C
230°C	210°C	190°C
240°C	220°C	200°C

AIR FRYER FAVOURITES COOKING GUIDE

Your air fryer is perfect for cooking all your favourite fresh ingredients in a healthy, delicious way! For those times when you need to rustle up a side of veggies, or fancy a back to basics dinner, we've put together a handy chart to help you get started.

Remember, these timings should be used as a guideline only! All air fryers are a little bit different, so take this chart as a starting point, and keep a close eye on your food as it cooks. Feel free to open the drawer or peek inside the basket to make sure you're on the way to crispy air-fried perfection!

VEGETABLES	TEMPERATURE	TIME
ASPARAGUS	200°C	6-8 MINUTES
AUBERGINE, SLICED	200°C	12-14 MINUTES
BEETROOT, QUARTERED	200°C	16-18 MINUTES
BROCCOLI	180°C	8-10 MINUTES
BRUSSELS SPROUTS	180°C	8-10 MINUTES
BUTTERNUT SQUASH, CUBED	200°C	18-20 MINUTES
CARROTS, SLICED	200°C	12-14 MINUTES
CAULIFLOWER	180°C	8-10 MINUTES
CORN ON THE COB	200°C	10-12 MINUTES
COURGETTE, SLICED	200°C	10-12 MINUTES
GREEN BEANS	200°C	8-10 MINUTES
MUSHROOMS	200°C	8-10 MINUTES
ONIONS, SLICED	180°C	10-12 MINUTES
PARSNIP, SLICED	200°C	16-18 MINUTES
PEPPERS, SLICED	200°C	8-10 MINUTES
SPRING ONIONS	200°C	6-8 MINUTES
TOMATOES, HALVED	180°C	6-8 MINUTES

POTATOES	TEMPERATURE	TIME
CHIPS AND WEDGES	200°C	20-25 MINUTES
JACKET POTATO	200°C	45-50 MINUTES
ROAST POTATOES	200°C	25-28 MINUTES
SWEET POTATO, WHOLE	200°C	35-40 MINUTES

MEAT & POULTRY	TEMPERATURE	TIME
BACON MEDALLIONS	200°C	5-7 MINUTES
SAUSAGES	180°C	12-15 MINUTES
CHICKEN BREASTS	180°C	18-20 MINUTES
CHICKEN THIGHS	180°C	20-22 MINUTES
WHOLE CHICKEN, MEDIUM	200°C	1 HOUR

FISH	TEMPERATURE	TIME
SALMON	180°C	10-12 MINUTES
PRAWNS	180°C	6-8 MINUTES
FISH CAKES	200°C	12-15 MINUTES
WHITE FISH	200°C	10-12 MINUTES

*These cooking times were tried and tested in our Dual Zone Air Fryer with a 9.5 litre capacity and 2470W of power.

BREAKFAST

BREAKFAST BAKE

🕐 10 MINS   🍲 10 MINS   ✕ SERVES 1

PER SERVING:
275 KCAL /12G CARBS

SPECIAL EQUIPMENT:
Large ovenproof ramekin (13.5 x 10 x 4cm/5¼ x 4 x 1½in)

2 bacon medallions
1 mushroom, sliced
2 tbsp baked beans
1 medium egg
10g reduced-fat
   Cheddar, grated
sea salt and freshly ground
   black pepper

TO ACCOMPANY *(optional)*
1 tbsp tomato ketchup
   (+22 kcal per tbsp)

Easy, cheesy and under 300 calories, these Breakfast Bakes will brighten up any morning! We've taken our favourite bits of a full English breakfast and used the air fryer to cut the cooking time down to just 10 minutes. Before you know it, you'll be digging into crispy bacon, mushroom, beans and egg, all topped with gooey melted cheese. You'll soon realize this recipe is too good to only enjoy for brekkie; it doubles up as a quick lunch or a speedy midweek dinner too!

Everyday Light

Add the bacon medallions and sliced mushroom to the air fryer basket. Air-fry at 220°C for 5 minutes, until the bacon is cooked through.

Remove the bacon and mushroom from the air fryer and place into an ovenproof ramekin. Spoon over the baked beans.

Gently make a well in the middle of the baked beans and crack the egg into it. Season the egg with salt and pepper. Sprinkle the cheese on top of the egg.

Place the ramekin in the air fryer and air-fry at 180°C for 5–6 minutes, depending on how firm you like your yolk. Use a tea towel or oven glove to carefully remove the ramekin from the air fryer (it will be very hot!) and serve.

TIP:

A little splash of Worcestershire sauce or Henderson's relish on top of the cheese before baking is a great addition! (This would add around 2 kcal per serving.)

FAN FAVOURITE

'Omg one of the best breakfasts ever & so filling'
Louisa Prince

VEGGIE

USE VEGETARIAN BACON ALTERNATIVE

VEGAN

OMIT THE BACON, USE PLANT-BASED YOGHURT

DAIRY FREE

USE PLANT-BASED YOGHURT

GLUTEN FREE

LOADED HASH BROWN

🕐 **10 MINS**   🍴 **20 MINS + 30 MINS COOLING**   ✕ **SERVES 1**

PER SERVING:
397 KCAL /56G CARBS

SPECIAL EQUIPMENT:
Microwave

1 baking potato, approx. 225g
¼ tsp onion granules
low-calorie cooking spray
1 bacon medallion
¼ avocado, peeled, stoned and sliced
1 tbsp fat-free Greek-style yoghurt
½ spring onion, trimmed and thinly sliced
1 tsp reduced-sugar sweet chilli sauce
sea salt and freshly ground black pepper

Forget avocado toast, breakfast is all about these crispy potato patties, stacked up with indulgent-tasting toppings. Our single-serve recipe is perfect for a weekend brunch, or those days when you fancy breakfast for dinner! The air fryer will take care of all the hard work, crisping up the outside of your hash brown while making sure the middle is nice and fluffy. We've topped ours with crunchy bacon, creamy avocado, Greek-style yoghurt and a drizzle of sweet chilli sauce, but you can play around with flavours, or swap in some vegetarian toppings if you prefer!

Everyday Light _____

Prick the potato a few times with a fork and place in the microwave. Microwave on High for about 4 minutes, or until it's just tender when pierced with a sharp knife. Take care not to cook the potato until it's too soft inside, as it still needs to be firm enough to grate. Remove from the microwave and leave to cool for about 30 minutes or until cool enough to handle.

Coarsely grate the cooled potato and its skin into a bowl. You can shred any bits of skin that are difficult to grate with a sharp knife. Add the onion granules, season with salt and pepper and stir gently to combine. Turn out onto a board and mould into a 12cm (5in) roughly-shaped patty.

Spray the air fryer basket with low-calorie cooking spray, making sure it completely covers the area where you will place the hash brown. Carefully lift the hash brown using a fish slice, and place in the air fryer, leaving space for the bacon.

Air-fry at 200°C for 10 minutes without moving the hash brown. This will ensure the base is crisp and firm before you turn it. After 10 minutes, carefully turn the hash brown over and place the bacon next to it. Spray both with low-calorie cooking spray and continue to cook for a further 5 minutes, turning the bacon halfway through. The hash brown should be crisp and golden brown, and the bacon cooked through.

Place the hash brown on a plate and dice the bacon. Arrange the avocado slices on top of the hash brown and add the bacon pieces. Top with a dollop of yoghurt, the spring onion and sweet chilli sauce.

TIP:

If you don't have a microwave, you can par-boil the whole potato in a saucepan of boiling water until it's just tender but not soft.

VEGGIE

USE VEGETARIAN
BACON
ALTERNATIVE

**LOW
CARB**

**DAIRY
FREE**

USE DF
CHEESE

**GLUTEN
FREE**

BACON *and* CHEESE FRITTATA

🕐 **10 MINS**　🍲 **25 MINS**　✗ **SERVES 2**

PER SERVING:
327 KCAL / 4.3G CARBS

SPECIAL EQUIPMENT:
Metal tin or disposable foil tray, no bigger than 22 x 16cm (8½ x 6in)

120g bacon medallions,
　cut into small squares
1 medium onion, peeled and
　finely chopped
low-calorie cooking spray
4 medium eggs
40g reduced-fat mature
　Cheddar, finely grated
1 tbsp chopped fresh chives
　(optional)
freshly ground black pepper

Breakfast is served! Whipping up a filling frittata has never been so easy, or so delicious. You can be creative with the fillings for this, but we love the simple combination of bacon, cheese and onion to kick-start the day. It's ideal if you have a fridge full of leftovers, then you could throw in any mushrooms, peppers or other veggies that need using up. Once the egg has set and the cheese has melted, there's only one decision left to make: will you eat it hot or cold? It's tasty either way!

Everyday Light

Place the bacon and onion into the metal tin or foil tray. Spray with low-calorie cooking spray.

Place in the air fryer, making sure there is at least a 2.5cm (1in) gap surrounding the tin or tray to allow for air flow. Air-fry at 200°C for 5 minutes, until the onions are soft and the bacon is starting to crisp.

While the bacon and onions are cooking, whisk the eggs in a bowl and add pepper to taste.

Pour the egg mixture over the bacon and onion and air-fry at 200°C for a further 15 minutes.

Sprinkle the cheese and chives (if using) over the top of the frittata and continue to cook for 3–5 minutes, until the cheese has melted.

Remove from the air fryer and enjoy warm, or leave to cool if you prefer to eat it cold.

BREAKFAST

SAUSAGE *and* EGG MUFFIN

🕐 **10 MINS**　　🍲 **20 MINS**　　✕ **SERVES 4**

FREEZE ME

PATTIES ONLY

BATCH COOK

DAIRY FREE

USE DF CHEESE

GLUTEN FREE

USE GF MUFFINS AND HENDERSON'S RELISH

PER SERVING:
413 KCAL /27G CARBS

SPECIAL EQUIPMENT:
4 x 150ml (5fl oz) ovenproof ramekins

400g 5%-fat pork mince
¼ tsp dried parsley
¼ tsp garlic granules
¼ tsp dried sage
½ tsp Henderson's relish (or Worcestershire sauce)
low-calorie cooking spray
4 medium eggs
4 wholemeal English muffins, sliced in half
4 light burger cheese slices
sea salt and freshly ground black pepper

TO ACCOMPANY *(optional)*
1 tbsp tomato ketchup
(+22 kcal per tbsp)

If you've been with us since our *Everyday Light* cookbook, these stacked breakfast muffins will look familiar! Just like the original, our air-fryer recipe is far lower in calories than the famous fast-food-chain version, without compromising on flavour. We've used lean pork mince to create juicy homemade sausage patties, and piled them high with light burger cheese slices on fluffy English muffins. Crack your eggs into ovenproof ramekins and they'll bake to perfection alongside your patties!

Weekly Indulgence

Place the pork mince, parsley, garlic granules, sage and Henderson's relish or Worcestershire sauce into a bowl. Season with salt and pepper. Mix until well combined (using your hands is best for this).

Shape into 4 equal-sized patties, each about 1.5cm (½in) thick. You can freeze the patties at this stage; just place them in a freezerproof container, separating them with pieces of non-stick baking paper, and place in the freezer. Before cooking, defrost overnight in the fridge and reshape.

Air-fry in 2 batches. Spray the air fryer basket with low-calorie cooking spray and add 2 patties, leaving space for 2 ramekins.

Air-fry at 180°C for 5 minutes. While they cook, spray 4 ramekins with low-calorie cooking spray and grease well. Crack an egg into each.

After 5 minutes, flip the patties and carefully place 2 of the ramekins containing the eggs into the basket. Cook for a further 4–5 minutes until the egg is cooked to your liking. Use an oven glove to remove the (very hot!) ramekins. Repeat with the 2 remaining patties and eggs.

Pop the muffins in the toaster and lightly toast.

Use a small knife to loosen the eggs in the ramekins. Place the sausage patties into the muffins, top with a cheese slice and then an egg. Repeat with the remaining 2 eggs and patties once cooked. Add the muffin lids and serve with some tomato ketchup or your favourite condiment!

FAN FAVOURITE

'Quick, easy, delicious!'
Iona Hall

VEGGIE

DAIRY FREE

USE DF CREAM CHEESE

GLUTEN FREE

USE GF BREAD

BANANA *and* RASPBERRY FRENCH TOAST

🕐 **10 MINS**   🍲 **6 MINS**   ✕ **SERVES 2**

PER SERVING:
366 KCAL / 51G CARBS

4 slices medium white bread, crusts removed
2 medium eggs
1 tsp vanilla extract
1 tsp granulated sweetener
4 tsp reduced-fat cream cheese
4 tsp maple syrup
2 small snack-size bananas
low-calorie cooking spray
8 raspberries, to garnish

If a slice of fruity French Toast sounds right up your street, you'll be pleased to hear this slimming-friendly version cooks in just 6 minutes per serving (thank you, air fryer!). Any time you fancy an indulgent breakfast or a quick-yet-decadent dessert, it's on your plate before you know it. The banana-filled bread is bathed in our vanilla-sweetened egg mixture and air-fried to golden perfection. All that's left to do is drizzle it with our maple syrup and cream cheese combo, sprinkle on the raspberries and enjoy!

Everyday Light —————————————

Using a bowl big enough to fit a slice of bread, beat the egg, vanilla and sweetener with a fork or balloon whisk until well mixed, then set aside.

Mix the cream cheese and maple syrup together in a small bowl, until it is free from any lumps. Set aside.

Put one and a half of the bananas in a bowl, mash roughly with a fork, then spread this over two slices of bread. Place the other slices of bread on top and press down firmly.

Carefully place the first 'sandwich' into the beaten egg mix. Leave until the bread has absorbed a quarter of the egg mixture, then flip it over for the other slice of bread to soak up a similar amount. Repeat for the second 'sandwich' while the first is cooking.

Spray the air fryer basket with low-calorie cooking spray. Carefully remove the first 'sandwich' from the bowl (it will be very soggy!) and place it in the air fryer. Air-fry for 3 minutes at 200°C. Carefully flip, then cook for another 3 minutes. It's ready when the bread is crisp and golden. Repeat with the second sandwich.

Place on a warm plate, slice the remaining piece of banana, then use to garnish the sandwiches along with the raspberries. Finally, drizzle with the cream cheese and maple syrup sauce and serve.

TIP:
Use white granulated sweetener that has the same weight, texture and sweetness as sugar.

BREAKFAST

CINNAMON BREAKFAST BUNS

⏱ **15 MINS**   🍲 **8 MINS + 20 MINS RESTING**   ✕ **MAKES 8**

PER BUN:
141 KCAL /26G CARBS

FOR THE BUNS
200g self-raising flour
100g fat-free Greek yoghurt
1 medium egg, beaten
3 tbsp granulated sweetener
1 tsp ground cinnamon
1 tsp vanilla extract
pinch of sea salt
low-calorie cooking spray

FOR THE FILLING
20g reduced-fat spread
2 tsp ground cinnamon
1 tsp granulated sweetener

FOR THE GLAZE
2 tbsp icing sugar
drop of vanilla extract
1½ tsp water

These lovely little Cinnamon Breakfast Buns will always get your day started on the right foot! While bakery-bought versions aren't the most slimming-friendly, our air-fried swirls are far lighter, at 141 calories each. It only takes a few minutes to roll and fill a whole batch, then you just leave them to bake and top them with a sticky-sweet glaze. The perfect, cosy companion to a frothy morning coffee, why not take things up a notch with a side of chopped fresh fruit?

Everyday Light

Put the bun ingredients in a bowl and knead to combine.

Mix the filling ingredients together in a separate small bowl.

Split the bun mixture into 8 equal pieces. Roll each piece into a thin sausage about 20cm (8in) long. Flatten slightly.

Split the filling equally into 8 and spread across the top of each flattened dough sausage. Gently shape the dough into spirals.

Line the air fryer drawer with non-stick baking paper and spray with low-calorie cooking spray. Place the buns in the lined drawer with space between them to expand. You may need to do this in batches, depending on the size of your air fryer.

Air-fry the buns at 170°C for 8 minutes. When the time has finished, leave them in the air fryer for a further 5 minutes while it is turned off.

Remove the buns from the air fryer and place on a wire rack. Leave for at least 15 minutes. While they are cooling, mix the glaze ingredients in a small bowl until smooth.

Once the buns have cooled, drizzle the buns with the glaze and serve.

TIP:
Use white granulated sweetener that has the same weight, texture and sweetness as sugar.

BREAKFAST

48

USE DF YOGHURT

USE GF OATS

PEACH MELBA BAKED OATS

🕐 **10 MINS**   🍲 **14 MINS + 5 MINS RESTING**   ✕ **SERVES 4**

PER SERVING:
173 KCAL /23G CARBS

SPECIAL EQUIPMENT:
Paper air fryer liners, or 18 x 18cm (7 x 7in) cake tin or silicone mould

2 medium eggs
100ml unsweetened almond milk
100g fat-free Greek-style yoghurt
1 tsp vanilla extract
2 tbsp granulated sweetener or sugar
100g porridge oats
1 small tin peaches in juice, drained (125g drained weight) and cut into small pieces
low-calorie cooking spray
50g fresh raspberries

TO ACCOMPANY (optional)
1 tbsp fat-free Greek yoghurt (+26 kcal per tbsp)

Creamy oats, juicy peaches and tart raspberries are a dreamy combo in this easy, batch-cookable breakfast recipe! To keep things budget-friendly, we've used tinned sweet peaches, rather than fresh fruit, to flavour our oats. Mixing in nutty almond milk and Greek yoghurt brings luxurious creaminess without adding lots of calories. The oat mixture will firm up as it bakes in the air fryer, making it ideal for portioning out to enjoy as a grab-and-go brekkie for the week ahead.

Everyday Light

In a large bowl, beat together the eggs, almond milk, yoghurt, vanilla extract and granulated sweetener or sugar.

Stir in the oats and peach pieces. Cover with a cloth and allow to rest for 5 minutes for the liquid to soak into the oats.

If you are using a tin, spray it with low-calorie cooking spray. If you are using a parchment liner, place it directly into the air fryer basket. Pour the oat mix into the tin or liner and dot the raspberries on top. Air-fry at 180°C for 12–14 minutes, until golden brown and firm to the touch. A skewer inserted into the middle should come out clean.

Cut into 4 portions and serve warm with some yoghurt, if you like, or allow to cool and wrap up portions for breakfast on the go. You can also freeze the baked oats in a freezerproof container once cold. Defrost overnight in the fridge, then reheat in the microwave for 2–3 minutes or in the air fryer at 180°C for 3–4 minutes.

TIPS:

Use white granulated sweetener that has the same weight, texture and sweetness as sugar.

Using sugar instead of sweetener will add 26 kcal per serving.

FAKEAWAYS

CHEESY GARLIC NAANZONE

🕐 **10 MINS**   🍲 **16 MINS + 45 MINS PROVING**   ✕ **SERVES 4**

PER SERVING:
324 KCAL /49G CARBS

250g white self-raising flour, plus extra for dusting
1 tsp caster sugar
½ tsp salt
½ tsp baking powder
4 garlic cloves, peeled and very finely chopped
250g fat-free natural yoghurt
oil, for greasing
60g reduced-fat Cheddar, finely grated
½ tsp garlic powder
1 tbsp chopped fresh coriander leaves
10g reduced-fat spread, melted

A cross between a garlic naan and a cheesy calzone, these are delicious dipped in Cheesy Roasted Vegetable Soup (page 160) or some mango chutney (add 48 kcal per tbsp). Our simple dough bakes to perfection in the air fryer, until it's bubbly and golden on the outside, with gooey cheese heaven in the middle – it'll be love at first bite!

Everyday Light

Sift the flour, sugar, salt and baking powder into a large bowl. Add the chopped garlic and stir in. Make a well in the centre and add the yoghurt. Using your fingertips, gradually draw the flour into the yoghurt, mixing to form a ball of soft dough.

Place the dough on a lightly floured surface and knead well for 5 minutes until the dough forms a smooth ball. You may need to flour the surface again.

Place the dough in a large, lightly greased bowl, cover with a large plate or clean tea towel and leave in a warm place for approx. 45 minutes, until the dough has increased slightly in size and feels a little puffy when pressed.

While the dough is proving, in another bowl, mix together the cheese, garlic powder and half of the coriander leaves.

After the dough has proved, turn it out onto a lightly floured surface and cut it into four equal pieces. If the dough is sticky, dust it with a little more flour. Using a rolling pin, gently roll a piece of dough into a 15cm (6in) diameter circle to create a wrap. Lay a quarter of the cheese and garlic filling over half of the wrap, making sure to leave a 1cm (½in) gap around the edge. Brush a little water around the edge. Fold the wrap in half, press down around the edge and crimp using the back of a fork. Repeat with the other three pieces of dough.

Line the air fryer basket with non-stick baking paper. Place the Naanzones into the basket, making sure they do not touch. Brush the tops of the Naanzones with the melted spread and air-fry at 160°C for 8 minutes.

With a pair of tongs, turn over the Naanzones and brush again with melted spread. Cook for a further 8 minutes and serve, with the remaining coriander scattered on top!

TIP:

If you want to freeze these, freeze in an air-tight container once cooled. Re-heat in the air fryer at 160°C for 5 minutes, or until hot throughout.

CHAR-SIU-STYLE PORK TENDERLOIN

🕐 **5 MINS***   🍲 **18 MINS****   ✕ **SERVES 3**

***+ 2 HOURS MARINATING **+ 5 MINS RESTING**

PER SERVING:
288 KCAL /9.7G CARBS

SPECIAL EQUIPMENT:
Pastry brush

1 pork tenderloin (fillet)
   approx. 500g
low-calorie cooking spray

FOR THE MARINADE
2 tbsp oyster sauce
1 tbsp soy sauce
1 tbsp honey
½ tsp Chinese 5-spice
2 garlic cloves, peeled and
   crushed
2cm (¾in) piece of root ginger,
   peeled and finely grated
½ tsp rice vinegar
a few drops of red food
   colouring (optional)

TO ACCOMPANY
50g nest egg noodles
   (+169 kcal per serving), 80g
   stir-fried vegetables (+43 kcal
   per serving), 2 tsp hoisin sauce
   (+43 kcal per serving)

This Char-Siu-Style Pork Tenderloin is succulent and rich with fakeaway flavour, thanks to a nifty homemade, sweet-yet-spicy marinade (trust us, it's worth waiting for the flavours to mingle!). We've added a few drops of food colouring to make our pork as red as takeaway versions, but there's nothing to stop you skipping this step – it'll taste just as delicious without! Once your tenderloin is cooked through with charred, smoky edges, it's ready to serve over egg noodles with colourful stir-fried vegetables and a light drizzle of hoisin sauce.

Special Occasion

Mix all the marinade ingredients together in a bowl.

Cut the pork tenderloin in half, so it will fit into your air fryer basket, and place in a non-metallic bowl. Smother the pork in the marinade, reserving about 2 tablespoons for basting. Rub into the pork so it is well coated. Cover and leave to marinate in the fridge for at least 2 hours.

Spray the air fryer basket with a little low-calorie cooking spray. Add the 2 pieces of pork to the basket and air-fry at 200°C for 7 minutes. Using a pastry brush, baste the top with the reserved marinade and flip over to baste the underside. Cook for a further 7 minutes.

Baste both sides again with any remaining marinade and cook for another 4 minutes, until thoroughly cooked. The pork should be sticky with charred BBQ-style edges.

Cover and allow to rest for 5 minutes, before cutting into thick slices and serving with egg noodles, stir-fried vegetables and hoisin sauce.

FAKEAWAYS

USE GF BREAD ROLLS

BBQ PULLED CHICKEN

🕐 **15 MINS**   🍲 **25 MINS**   ✕ **SERVES 4**

PER SERVING:
186 KCAL /9.1G CARBS

SPECIAL EQUIPMENT:
18cm (7in) square cake tin or silicone mould

500g skinless, boneless chicken breasts, cut into 5cm (2in) chunks
low-calorie cooking spray

FOR THE BBQ SPICE MIX
2 tsp smoked sweet paprika
1 tsp garlic granules
1 tsp dried oregano
1 tsp mustard powder
1 tsp granulated sweetener or sugar

FOR THE SAUCE
150g passata
2 tsp tomato puree
1 tsp onion granules
1 tbsp Henderson's relish
1 tbsp runny honey
2 tsp balsamic vinegar
sea salt and freshly ground black pepper

TO ACCOMPANY
60g wholemeal bread roll (+146 kcal per serving) and 75g mixed salad (+15 kcal per serving)

TIPS:
This is a versatile dish. Serve it in a bread roll with heaps of fresh salad, or use it to fill one of our Fluffy Jacket Potatoes (page 140).

You can substitute Henderson's relish with Worcestershire sauce, but that does contain gluten and fish.

With sweetness from the honey, smokiness from the paprika and tanginess from balsamic vinegar, our quick-to-make BBQ sauce will keep you coming back for more! Luckily, we've used chicken breast for this recipe, which is far leaner than pork, so you can load up your plate for fewer calories. Your air fryer will make light work of cooking the chicken until it's tender and easy to shred, so all you have to do is decide how to serve it. Stuff it inside a sandwich, pile it on a salad, or spoon it inside a Fluffy Jacket Potato (page 140) – the options are endless!

Everyday Light

Mix all the BBQ spice mix ingredients together in a small bowl.

Spray the chicken chunks with low-calorie cooking spray and sprinkle over 1 tablespoon of the spice mix. Rub evenly into the chicken.

Depending on your style of air fryer, either place the chicken pieces into the drawer (after removing the basket) or place in the cake tin or silicone mould. Air-fry at 180°C for 12 minutes, turning the chicken halfway through.

Meanwhile, mix together the sauce ingredients and add the remaining spice mix.

After 12 minutes, stir the sauce through the chicken pieces and air-fry for another 10–12 minutes. The chicken should be cooked through with no pink remaining.

Transfer the chicken and sauce from the air fryer into a bowl and shred the chicken pieces using 2 forks. Stir well so the sauce coats the shredded chicken and serve.

For freezing and reheating guidelines see page 17.

FAKEAWAYS

ZINGER BURGERS

🕐 **10 MINS**   🍲 **15 MINS**   ✕ **SERVES 2**

PER SERVING:
356 KCAL /29G CARBS

SPECIAL EQUIPMENT:
Food bag, meat tenderizer or rolling pin

20g chilli tortilla chips
1 tsp chilli powder
1 tsp garlic granules
1 tsp paprika
1 large skinless, boneless
   chicken breast, approx. 250g
1 tsp plain flour
1 small egg, beaten
low-calorie cooking spray
2 wholemeal burger buns
lettuce leaves, to serve

TO ACCOMPANY *(optional)*
1 tbsp reduced-fat mayonnaise
   (+40 kcal per tbsp)

You'll want to add the ingredients for these unbelievably crispy Zinger Burgers to your next shopping list! Piled high on wholemeal buns, with lettuce leaves and your choice of sauce (we'd go for light mayo or homemade salsa), they're far lighter than you'd expect at less than 400 calories each. Forget about breadcrumbs – we've smashed together fiery tortilla chips, flour and a simple blend of store-cupboard spices instead. You can trust your air fryer to keep the chicken breasts nice and juicy, while the zingy coating bakes until it looks and tastes like it's been deep-fried at a restaurant.

Everyday Light ─────────────────────

In a sealable food bag, combine the tortilla chips and spices. Use a rolling pin to break them down into a crumb. Tip out onto a plate.

Put the chicken breast into another sealable food bag. Use the rolling pin to flatten out the thick end so that the whole breast is an even thickness (around 2cm/¾in). Make sure the chicken breast is dry and cut it into 2 equal halves. Place the flour on one plate and the beaten egg on a separate plate. Dust the chicken lightly with the flour and then dip it into the egg. Dip the chicken breast pieces into the crumb to coat the tops, using any remaining crumbs to coat the bottoms.

Spray the inside of the air fryer basket with low-calorie cooking spray. Place the coated chicken pieces inside and spray the tops with some more low-calorie cooking spray. Air-fry at 180°C for 15 minutes, flipping the chicken halfway through.

Check the chicken is cooked and white throughout before assembling the burgers with the lettuce and buns.

For freezing and reheating guidelines see page 17.

FAKEAWAYS

TEX MEX-STYLE CHICKEN

🕐 **5 MINS**   🍲 **20 MINS**   ✕ **SERVES 4**

PER SERVING:
421 KCAL /17G CARBS

SPECIAL EQUIPMENT:
Food bag, meat tenderizer or rolling pin

1 x 300g jar salsa
40g reduced-fat
   Cheddar, grated
80g chilli tortilla chips
4 small skinless, boneless
   chicken breasts, approx.
   175g each
1 egg, beaten
low-calorie cooking spray

TO ACCOMPANY
75g mixed salad
   (+15 kcal per serving)

Those of you who are already familiar with our classic Zinger Burger recipe will know we LOVE using tortilla chips to hack our way to a lighter crunchy coating for air-fried chicken (you'll find the Zinger on page 60). For a Tex Mex-inspired twist, each chicken breast is stuffed with gooey reduced-fat Cheddar and tangy salsa – and you'll have to bite through a fiery layer of crushed-up chilli tortilla chips to get to it! It's ready in a jiffy, courtesy of your air fryer (just 20 minutes!), even if it looks and tastes like you've popped to the drive-thru.

Weekly Indulgence

In a bowl, mix together the salsa and cheese to make the filling for the chicken.

Place the tortilla chips into a food bag and smash until they are nearly all in a fine crumb. Set aside in a bowl.

Place the chicken breasts on a chopping board and gently pound with a meat tenderizer or rolling pin to flatten each breast a little – don't make them too thin.

Make a pocket in each chicken breast by using the tip of a sharp knife to make a lengthways slit, then use your fingers to widen the pocket. Make sure to not slice all the way through the chicken. Place a quarter of the filling into each chicken pocket.

Add the beaten egg to a bowl. Take a piece of chicken and dip it into the beaten egg, then place it in the bowl containing the crushed tortilla chips. Toss the chicken around in the bowl to make sure it is fully coated with the crumb mix on both sides. Repeat with the remaining three breasts.

Spray the inside of the air fryer basket with low-calorie cooking spray. Place the chicken into the air fryer and spray with low-calorie cooking spray. Air-fry at 180°C for 20 minutes, turning half way through, until the chicken is crispy. Serve with a mixed salad.

To freeze, once cool freeze in an air-tight container. Re-heat in the air fryer at 180°C for 5–8 minutes, or until piping hot throughout.

FAKEAWAYS

VEGGIE

FREEZE ME
SAUCE ONLY

BATCH COOK

DAIRY FREE

SWEET POTATO KATSU

🕐 **20 MINS**   🍲 **45 MINS**   ✕ **SERVES 4**

PER SERVING:
328KCAL /60G CARBS

SPECIAL EQUIPMENT:
Stick blender or food processor

1 medium egg, beaten
35g panko breadcrumbs
400g sweet potatoes,
   peeled and cut into 5mm
   (¼in)-thick slices
sea salt and freshly ground
   black pepper
Lime slices, to serve (optional)

FOR THE CURRY SAUCE
low-calorie cooking spray
250g onions, peeled and
   chopped
4 garlic cloves, peeled
   and crushed
2 tbsp curry powder
1 tbsp garam masala
400g carrots, peeled and
   roughly chopped
200g potatoes, peeled and
   roughly chopped
750ml vegetable stock
   (2 veg stock cubes dissolved
   in 750ml boiling water)
1 tbsp granulated sweetener
2 tbsp soy sauce
2 tbsp garlic granules
1 tbsp onion granules
pinch of salt

TO ACCOMPANY
125g cooked basmati rice
   (+173 kcal per serving)

TIP:

Use white granulated sweetener
that has the same weight,
texture and sweetness as sugar.

It's a fact of life that everything tastes better when it's smothered in creamy, mild katsu curry sauce. Sweet potatoes are healthy and filling, so they make a great vegetarian substitute when you fancy a meat-free dinner. Just like if you were making chicken katsu, these slices of sweet potato get coated in panko breadcrumbs, ready to be crisped up in the air fryer. When they're crunchy and golden, nestle them in the sauce and add some lime wedges to serve.

Special Occasion ─────────────

Spray a saucepan with low-calorie cooking spray and place over a medium heat. Add the onions and sauté for 6–8 minutes, until softened and lightly coloured. Add the crushed garlic, curry powder and garam masala and cook for another minute until fragrant.

Add the remaining sauce ingredients and bring to the boil. Reduce the heat to a simmer and cook for 45 minutes, stirring occasionally and making sure it does not reduce too much.

While the sauce cooks, prepare the sweet potatoes. Season the egg with some salt and pepper in a bowl. Place the breadcrumbs in another large bowl. Dip each slice of sweet potato first into the egg, then into the bowl of breadcrumbs. Toss around to coat well.

Place the sweet potato slices into the air fryer basket and spray with low-calorie cooking spray. You may need to do this in batches, depending on the size of your air fryer. Air-fry at 200°C for 15–20 minutes until crisp and golden.

When the carrots and potatoes are soft, remove the pan from the heat and blitz the sauce using a stick blender or a food processor. Check the consistency. You can add a little more water if it is too thick. If it is too thin, pour back into the pan and return to the stove to reduce. Keep an eye on it and stir to prevent it catching.

When the sweet potatoes are cooked, serve with the sauce and some boiled rice, with lime slices too if you like.

For freezing and reheating guidelines see page 17.

FAKEAWAYS

VEGGIE

USE VEGAN
FISH SAUCE

VEGAN

USE VEGAN FISH
SAUCE, AGAVE
SYRUP INSTEAD
OF HONEY

DAIRY
FREE

STICKY TERIYAKI AUBERGINE

🕐 **10 MINS**   🍲 **15 MINS**   ✕ **SERVES 4**

PER SERVING:
69 KCAL / 11G CARBS

SPECIAL EQUIPMENT:
Pastry brush

2 aubergines (500g), sliced into quarters lengthways
low-calorie cooking spray
sesame seeds, toasted (optional)
spring onion, finely sliced (optional)

FOR THE TERIYAKI GLAZE
2 tbsp dark soy sauce
1 tbsp white wine vinegar
2 tbsp tomato puree
3 tbsp runny honey
½ tsp dried chilli flakes
1 tbsp fish sauce
2 garlic cloves, peeled and finely grated
1 tbsp finely grated root ginger
zest and juice of 1 lime

TO ACCOMPANY *(optional)*
125g cooked basmati rice
(+173 kcal per serving)

We couldn't cram more flavour into these Sticky Teriyaki Aubergines if we tried! Raid your cupboards and you'll probably find most of the ingredients you need to make the sticky, sweet, tangy and salty teriyaki glaze. It does call for fish sauce, which is the only thing that makes this recipe not vegetarian – you can swap this for a vegan 'fish' sauce if you prefer! Delicious with a simple side of rice, we also love to pair this dish with our Brocauli Bites from page 166.

Everyday Light ————————————————

Place the aubergine quarters into the air fryer basket and spray with low-calorie cooking spray. Air-fry at 200°C for 8 minutes. Check that the aubergine is soft and cooked all the way through, if not, cook for a further 2 minutes.

While the aubergines are cooking, place all of the glaze ingredients into a bowl and mix well.

Once the aubergines are cooked, use a pastry brush to brush them with the teriyaki glaze, making sure they are well coated. Air-fry at 180°C for 5 minutes until the teriyaki sauce takes on a sticky consistency.

Remove from the air fryer and sprinkle over some toasted sesame seeds and sliced spring onion, if using. Serve with rice, or your choice of accompaniment.

FAKEAWAYS

SHISH KEBAB

🕐 **20 MINS**　🍲 **10 MINS**　✕ **SERVES 4**

FREEZE ME

MEAT KEBAB MIX ONLY

BATCH COOK

MEAT KEBAB MIX ONLY

DAIRY FREE

USE DF YOGHURT

GLUTEN FREE

PER SERVING:
263 KCAL /15G CARBS

SPECIAL EQUIPMENT:
8 skewers (wooden or metal) to fit your air fryer

400g 5%-fat beef mince
1 tsp onion powder
1 tsp garlic powder
½ tsp dried mint
1 tsp ground coriander
½ tsp dried chilli flakes
1 tsp ground cumin
pinch of salt

FOR THE VEG KEBABS
2 medium tomatoes, cut in half
2 peppers, any colour, deseeded and cut into 12 pieces
2 small courgettes, each cut into 6 slices
1 red onion, peeled and cut into 8 wedges
4 mushrooms
½ tsp garlic powder
½ tsp chilli powder
pinch of salt
low-calorie cooking spray

FOR THE YOGHURT SAUCE
1 tsp mint sauce (or ½ tsp dried mint)
60g fat-free Greek yoghurt

TO ACCOMPANY
75g mixed salad
(+15 kcal per serving)

Step away from the takeaway menu and turn on your air fryer instead! It only takes half an hour to rustle up these scrummy Shish Kebabs, made with low-fat beef mince and our easy blend of seasonings. For added flavour, we've included skewers of fresh vegetables to serve with your kebab, along with a dollop of creamy, mint-infused yoghurt. All you need to add is a side salad to turn this into a fakeaway feast!

Everyday Light ─────────────────

First, make the four veg kebabs. On each of four of the skewers put the following: 1 tomato half, 3 pepper pieces, 3 courgette slices, 2 onion wedges and 1 mushroom. In a small bowl, mix together the garlic, chilli and salt and sprinkle over the kebabs. Set aside.

Put the beef mince into a bowl, then add the onion powder, garlic powder, dried mint, coriander, chilli flakes, cumin and salt. Mix well.

Knead the mince, like a dough, to distribute the spices evenly. Split the mince into 4 and roll them into sausage shapes.

Spray the inside of the air fryer basket with low-calorie cooking spray. Skewer each 'sausage' with the remaining four skewers, then carefully place both the meat and veg kebabs in the basket and air-fry at 200°C for 8–10 minutes. Turn the meat kebabs halfway through cooking. Don't turn the veg kebabs as they are likely to fall apart if you handle them too much.

While the kebabs are cooking, mix the mint sauce, or dried mint, with the yoghurt.

Remove the kebabs from the air fryer and serve 1 meat and 1 veg kebab per portion. Drizzle with the mint yoghurt and serve with a side salad.

For freezing and reheating guidelines see page 17.

FAKEAWAYS

VEGGIE

VEGAN

DAIRY FREE

GLUTEN FREE

SALT *and* PEPPER CHIPS

🕐 **10 MINS + 10 MINS SOAKING**   🍲 **30 MINS**   ✕ **SERVES 2**

PER SERVING:
370 KCAL /77G CARBS

800g potatoes, cut into
  1cm (½in)-thick chips
  (no need to peel)
low-calorie cooking spray
½ green pepper, deseeded
  and diced
½ red pepper, deseeded
  and diced
1–2 whole chillies, deseeded
  and diced
1–2 spring onions, trimmed
  and finely diced

FOR THE SPICE MIX
1 tbsp sea salt flakes
1 tbsp granulated sweetener
½ tbsp Chinese 5-spice
1 tsp ground white pepper
½ tsp dried chilli flakes

TIPS:

Use white granulated
sweetener that has the
same weight, texture and
sweetness as sugar.

You can peel your potatoes
if you prefer, just make sure
you end up with 800g of
prepared potatoes.

FAN FAVOURITE

'Deliciously guilt free!'
Ashlee Hutchinson

Let's face it, there's absolutely no way this cookbook would be complete without a page dedicated to Salt and Pepper Chips! An elite takeaway favourite, we've recreated the flavours you'd expect from nipping to the chippy by rustling up our own slimming-friendly spice mix (it's the perfect blend of savoury sea salt and fiery chilli!). Toss it all together with evenly-cut chips and let your air fryer do the hard work for you. Our top tip for this recipe? Shake, shake, shake! It'll get your chips gloriously crispy all over, ready to be mixed with colourful chopped peppers and spring onions.

Everyday Light

Place the chips in a large bowl and cover with cold water. Soak for 10 minutes to remove the starch (this will produce a crispier chip).

While the chips soak, mix together the ingredients for the spice mix in a small bowl. You won't need all of it for this recipe, so save some for another day in a small airtight container.

When the chips have soaked, drain them well and pat dry with a clean tea towel. Return them to a dry bowl and spray well with low-calorie cooking spray. Season with 2 teaspoons of the spice mix and toss to coat evenly.

Add the seasoned chips to the air fryer basket. Air-fry at 200°C for 20 minutes, giving the basket a good shake throughout to ensure even cooking.

Add the diced peppers and chillies and cook for another 5 minutes. Then add the diced spring onion and cook for a final 5 minutes.

Check that the chips are cooked and golden brown before serving.

PIZZA TURKEY BURGERS

🕐 **15 MINS**   🍲 **25 MINS**   ✕ **SERVES 6**

PER SERVING:
372 KCAL /42G CARBS

FOR THE KETCHUP
400g passata
1 tsp garlic granules
1 tsp onion granules
1 tsp dried mixed Italian herbs
1 tbsp balsamic vinegar
1 tsp granulated sweetener
   (or sugar)
sea salt and freshly ground
   black pepper

FOR THE BURGERS
1 small courgette, grated
500g turkey breast mince
1 tsp garlic granules
1 tsp onion granules
20g panko breadcrumbs
1 medium egg, beaten
a good handful of fresh basil
   leaves, chopped
low-calorie cooking spray

TO SERVE
120g reduced-fat mozzarella,
   cut into 6 slices
6 ciabatta rolls, sliced open
mixed salad leaves
1 red onion, peeled and sliced
2 tomatoes, sliced

TO ACCOMPANY *(optional)*
75g mixed salad
   (+15 kcal per serving)

TIP:

Use white granulated sweetener that has the same weight, texture and sweetness as sugar.

Please don't make us choose between a pizza or a burger! We can't pick favourites, so we've combined them into one easy recipe instead. These homemade turkey burgers are far juicier than shop-bought versions, thanks to the sneaky grated courgette we've hidden inside them. Melt some mozzarella on top of each patty, before loading them inside Italian-inspired ciabatta rolls with a good dollop of our pizza-style ketchup. We're warning you now, the ketchup is so moreish that you'll want extra for dipping!

Everyday Light ———————————————

Place all the ketchup ingredients into a saucepan and set over a medium heat. Cook for around 15 minutes, stirring occasionally, until it has reduced to the consistency of ketchup. Transfer into a bowl.

Place the grated courgette into a clean tea towel and squeeze out as much liquid as you can. Place in a bowl with the remaining burger ingredients and mix well. Hands are best for this. Divide into 6 and shape into equal-sized patties about 2cm (¾in) thick.

Spray the inside of the air fryer basket with low-calorie cooking spray and carefully place in the burgers, leaving enough space between them for air to circulate. Spray the tops with low-calorie cooking spray and air-fry at 200°C for 8 minutes. You may need to do this in batches.

Open the basket and add a slice of mozzarella to the top of each burger. Cook for a further 1–2 minutes until the mozzarella is bubbling and the burgers are fully cooked.

Fill the ciabatta rolls with mixed leaves, onion and tomato slices, place a burger inside and top with the ketchup. Serve with a mixed salad, if you like.

If freezing cooked, wrap individually and store in a freezer-proof bag. Defrost overnight in the fridge and reheat in a moderate oven until piping hot. If freezing uncooked, shape into rough burger patties and wrap well. Store in a freezer-proof bag. Defrost overnight in the fridge. Reshape into burgers and cook as per instructions.

FAKEAWAYS

USE GF STOCK CUBE

MADRAS MEATBALLS

🕐 **20 MINS**   🍲 **45 MINS**   ✕ **SERVES 4**

PER SERVING:
296 KCAL /16G CARBS

SPECIAL EQUIPMENT:
Silicone liner or foil tray approx.
22 x 16cm (8½ x 6in)

FOR THE MEATBALLS
500g 5%-fat beef mince
½ tsp garlic granules
1 tsp onion granules
½ tsp garam masala
¼ tsp salt
¼ tsp freshly ground black pepper
1 medium egg, beaten

FOR THE MADRAS SAUCE
low-calorie cooking spray
2 medium onions, peeled and
   finely chopped
1 red pepper, deseeded and diced
1 green pepper, deseeded and
   diced
4 garlic cloves, peeled and crushed
3cm (1¼in) piece of root ginger,
   peeled and finely grated
1 medium green chilli, seeds left
   in and finely chopped (ours
   weighed 8g)
1 tsp mild chilli powder
1 tsp ground turmeric
2 tsp ground cumin
2 tsp ground coriander
1 tbsp garam masala
½ tsp ground cinnamon
1 x 400g tin chopped tomatoes
2 tbsp tomato puree
400ml beef stock (1 beef stock
   cube dissolved in 400ml boiling
   water)
3 tbsp cider vinegar
1 tsp salt
1 tsp granulated sweetener
   or sugar

If you enjoy our Beef Madras and you're a fan of meatballs, you're in luck! Our Madras Meatballs bring the best of both dishes to the table. A great alternative to a takeaway, you can have your meatballs sizzling away in the air fryer while you simmer the sauce on the hob. Once it's all put together, you'll finish it off in the air fryer, until it's ready to dish up with a fluffy portion of rice. This Madras sauce turns out medium-hot, but (as always!) it's easy to add more or less chilli to get just the right amount of fiery flavour.

Weekly Indulgence ───────────────

In a mixing bowl, add the beef mince, garlic granules, onion granules, garam masala, salt and black pepper and mix until well combined. Add the egg a little at a time (you may not need to use all the egg, depending on its size) and combine until the mixture holds together firmly enough to form meatballs. Shape the mixture into 12 evenly-sized meatballs.

Put the meatballs on a plate and place in the fridge while you make the Madras sauce.

Spray a large frying pan with low-calorie cooking spray and place over a medium heat. Add the onions, peppers, garlic, ginger and green chilli and cook gently for 5–10 minutes, stirring, until softened and golden.

Add the chilli powder, turmeric, cumin, ground coriander, garam masala and cinnamon to the frying pan. Stir and cook gently for 2–3 minutes.

Add the chopped tomatoes, tomato puree, beef stock, vinegar, salt and sweetener or sugar. Stir until well mixed. Lower the heat and simmer gently, uncovered, for 15 minutes until the sauce has reduced and thickened.

While the sauce is simmering, place the meatballs into the air fryer basket and air-fry at 200°C for 10 minutes until the meatballs are golden brown.

Remove the meatballs from the air fryer and, using tongs, carefully place them into the silicone liner or foil tray. When the sauce is cooked, pour it over the meatballs.

FAKEAWAYS

TO GARNISH *(optional)*
a few fresh coriander leaves,
roughly chopped

TO ACCOMPANY
125g cooked basmati rice
(+173 kcal per serving)

Place the liner or tray back into the air fryer and air-fry at 200°C for 15 minutes, stirring halfway through.

Sprinkle with a few chopped coriander leaves, if you like, and serve with basmati rice.

For freezing and reheating guidelines see page 17.

LOADED CHEESEBURGER FRIES

⏱ **15 MINS + 10 MINS SOAKING**   🍲 **30 MINS**   ✕ **SERVES 4**

VEGGIE

USE QUORN MINCE, AND VEGETABLE STOCK

FREEZE ME

BURGER TOPPING ONLY

GLUTEN FREE

USE GF STOCK CUBE

PER SERVING:
466 KCAL /45G CARBS

FOR THE FRIES
800g potatoes, cut into 1cm (½in)-
thick fries (no need to peel)
low-calorie cooking spray
pinch of salt

FOR THE BURGER TOPPING
500g 5%-fat beef mince
1 tsp onion granules
1 tsp garlic granules
1 tsp tomato puree
2 tsp Henderson's relish
100ml beef stock (1 beef stock
cube dissolved in 100ml
boiling water)

FOR THE BURGER SAUCE
50g reduced-fat mayonnaise
50g fat-free natural yoghurt
¼ tsp mustard powder
1 tsp tomato puree
1 tbsp pickling juice

TO SERVE
100g Cheddar, grated
1 red onion, peeled and sliced
2 tomatoes, diced
2 dill pickles, sliced

TO ACCOMPANY *(optional)*
75g mixed salad
(+15 kcal per serving)

TIP:

Use this recipe to make fries
to accompany your favourite
meals! Air Fryer Fries are 169
calories per portion.

Bring drive-through flavours to the table with a little help from your air fryer! Even if you leave off the cheeseburger-inspired toppings, this is the ultimate recipe for golden, crispy homemade fries. Don't skip the step of soaking the spuds for 10 minutes before throwing them into the air fryer basket – it's the key to crunchy on the outside, fluffy in the middle perfection.

Weekly Indulgence ―――――――――――

Place the fries in a large bowl and cover with cold water. Soak for 10 minutes to remove the starch (this will produce a crispier fry). Drain the fries well and pat dry with a clean tea towel. Return to a dry bowl and spray well with low-calorie cooking spray. Sprinkle on a little salt to taste. Toss to coat evenly.

Add the fries to the air fryer basket and air-fry at 200°C for 25–30 minutes, giving the basket a good shake every 10 minutes to ensure even cooking.

While the fries cook, make your cheeseburger topping. Place a frying pan over a high heat. When hot, add the mince and cook for 5 minutes until browned. Stir in the onion granules, garlic granules, tomato puree, Henderson's relish and stock. Cook for 2–3 minutes until the sauce has reduced and thickened and coats the mince like a glaze.

You can freeze the beef mince at this stage. Cool quickly, then freeze in an airtight container as soon as possible. Defrost overnight in the fridge, then reheat by spraying a frying pan with low-calorie cooking spray and placing it over a medium heat, then add the mince and a tablespoon of water. Stir until piping hot throughout.

Mix together all the sauce ingredients. You can thin it down with a few tablespoons of water if you prefer it runnier.

When the fries are cooked, distribute among 4 bowls. Top with the mince and sprinkle over the cheese.

Top with the red onion, tomatoes, dill pickles and drizzle over the burger sauce.

FAKEAWAYS

FREEZE ME

BATCH COOK

DAIRY FREE

GLUTEN FREE

USE GF SOY SAUCE

KUNG PAO PORK

🕐 **10 MINS**　🍲 **25 MINS**　✕ **SERVES 4**

PER SERVING:
301 KCAL /33G CARBS

SPECIAL EQUIPMENT:
Parchment paper or
air fryer liner

FOR THE PORK
400g lean diced pork
2 tbsp cornflour
1 tsp Chinese 5-spice
1 tsp toasted sesame oil

FOR THE SAUCE
low-calorie cooking spray
1 small onion, peeled and thinly
　sliced
1 medium red pepper, deseeded
　and diced
1 medium carrot, peeled and
　thinly sliced into strips
2 garlic cloves, peeled and
　crushed
1 x 225g tin bamboo shoots,
　drained
1 tbsp brown sugar
3 tbsp granulated sweetener
60ml cider vinegar
1 tbsp runny honey
2 tsp dried chilli flakes
2 tbsp tomato puree
1 tbsp dark soy sauce
2 spring onions, trimmed and
　thinly sliced, to garnish

TO ACCOMPANY
125g cooked basmati rice
　(+173 kcal per serving)

TIP:

Use white granulated sweetener
that has the same weight, texture
and sweetness as sugar.

For us, there's no better feeling than putting a slimming-friendly spin on a classic takeaway favourite! You might have tried our oven-baked Kung Pao Pork before, but this air-fryer method is about to show you a whole new level of crispiness. When the pork strips are tender with a golden crunch, they only need a minute in a pan with our homemade sweet and salty, Chinese-inspired sauce. We can promise you'll get that 'eating out' feeling for a fraction of the calories . . . Time to grab your chopsticks!

Weekly Indulgence ————————————————

Line the air fryer with parchment paper or an air fryer liner.

Place the pork, cornflour, Chinese 5-spice and sesame oil into a sandwich bag, seal the bag and shake until the pork is completely coated in the cornflour mix. Spread across the parchment or liner in the air fryer. Air-fry the pork at 180°C for 25 minutes, turning halfway.

While the pork is cooking, make the sauce. Spray a frying pan with low-calorie cooking spray and sauté the onion, red pepper and carrot, over a low heat, until they start to soften. This will take 6–7 minutes.

Once the vegetables have softened, add the garlic and bamboo shoots and cook for a further 2 minutes, stirring frequently.

Add all of the remaining sauce ingredients (except the spring onions), mix well to combine and simmer over a low heat for 10–15 minutes until the sauce has thickened and reduced.

You can freeze at this stage by freezing the sauce and the cooked meat separately. For standard reheating guidelines see page 17.

Once the pork is cooked, crisp and golden, add it to the sauce and stir. Serve immediately with rice or your choice of accompaniment, and garnish with the thinly sliced spring onions.

FAKEAWAYS

GOCHUJANG CHICKEN NUGGETS

🕐 **10 MINS** 🍲 **15 MINS** ✕ **SERVES 4**

PER SERVING:
233 KCAL /22G CARBS

40g panko breadcrumbs
1 tsp fine garlic granules
1 medium egg, beaten
3 medium skinless, boneless
   chicken breasts, approx. 140g
   each, cut into 3cm (1in) chunks
low-calorie cooking spray
sea salt and freshly ground
   black pepper

FOR THE GOCHUJANG SAUCE
3 tbsp mild gochujang paste
2 tbsp runny honey
2 tsp dark soy sauce
¼ tsp fine garlic granules

FOR THE TOP
2 tsp chopped fresh chives
½ tsp sesame seeds

TO ACCOMPANY
125g cooked basmati rice
   (+173 kcal per serving)

TIPS:

Gochujang paste is a spicy Korean
red chilli paste that has a savoury,
umami richness and a slightly
sweet and smoky flavour. It comes
in varying levels of chilli heat; we
used a mild paste, but you can use
a hotter one if you prefer. You can
find it in larger supermarkets or
Asian grocery stores.

Make sure to use fine garlic
granules as these will stick well
to the chicken nuggets.

You can't say no to chicken nuggets, especially when they
come with this sticky, spicy, sweet, smoky sauce! Gochujang
is a popular Korean ingredient, made from red chillies and
fermented soybeans. We've used it to make a quick glaze
for our air-fried nuggs, which gets drizzled over the crispy
chicken right before serving. Thanks to the magic of your
air fryer, you'll get all of the crunch of a deep-fried version,
for a fraction of the calories!

Weekly Indulgence ———————————————

Place the panko breadcrumbs on a plate, add the garlic
granules and season well with salt and pepper. Mix with
clean fingers until completely combined.

Place the beaten egg on another plate. Dip the chicken
pieces in the egg to coat all over, then into the breadcrumbs
until completely coated.

Place the coated chicken pieces in a single layer in the air
fryer basket, leaving space between each one. Spray the
tops with low-calorie cooking spray and air-fry at 170°C
for 15 minutes, turning the nuggets over halfway through
and spraying again. You may need to do this in batches,
depending on the size of your air fryer. Cook until crisp and
golden. There should be no signs of pinkness in the middle
and the juices should run clear.

You can freeze the chicken nuggets before cooking (open
freeze on a tray then pack into a freezerproof container) or
after cooking (simply place in a freezerproof container once
cold). Defrost thoroughly in the fridge before cooking or
reheating in the oven.

While the chicken nuggets are cooking, make the gochujang
sauce. Place the gochujang paste, honey, soy sauce and
garlic granules in a small bowl and mix until combined.

Just before serving, drizzle the gochujang sauce over
the cooked chicken nuggets, sprinkle with the chopped
chives and sesame seeds. Serve with basmati rice or
accompaniment of your choice.

USE GF PANKO
BREADCRUMBS

FISH *and* CHIPS FISHCAKES

🕐 **20 MINS + 30 MINS CHILLING**   🍲 **30 MINS**   ✕ **SERVES 6**

PER SERVING:
185 KCAL /17G CARBS

SPECIAL EQUIPMENT:
Potato masher

200g potato, peeled and
   cut into chunks
400g cod fillets, skinless
   and boneless
150ml cold water
100ml skimmed milk
150g frozen peas, defrosted
¼ tsp garlic granules
2 tbsp finely chopped fresh
   chives
zest and juice of ½ lemon
2 medium eggs, beaten
80g panko breadcrumbs
low-calorie cooking spray
sea salt and freshly ground
   black pepper

TO SERVE
2 tbsp reduced-fat mayonnaise
1 tbsp tartare sauce
1 tbsp lemon juice

TO ACCOMPANY *(optional)*
75g mixed salad (+15 kcal
   per serving), 1 tbsp tomato
   ketchup (+15 kcal per
   tablespoon)

TIPS:

Don't mash the peas too much,
they need to stay quite chunky.

If you want to freeze these,
wrap individually and freeze
once cooled. Defrost and
reheat in the air fryer for 5-8
minutes to keep them crisp.
Handle carefully as they
can become fragile when
defrosted.

These Fish and Chips Fishcakes were made for Friday nights! We've taken all the best bits of a chippy tea, rolled them into tasty panko-breadcrumbed patties and popped them in the air fryer until they're gorgeous and golden. All you need is a dollop of our lemony mayo and tartare sauce to round off all the chip-shop flavours on your plate.

Everyday Light ————————————————

Add the potato to a pan of cold salted water. Bring to the boil over a medium heat and cook for 8–10 minutes until soft. Drain well, mash and leave to one side to cool slightly.

While the potato cooks, place the cod fillets in a saucepan, and pour over the water and milk. Cover with a lid and set the saucepan over a medium heat. Bring to the boil then lower the heat and simmer for 5 minutes. Remove the pan from the heat and leave covered for 5 more minutes.

Add the peas to a small bowl and roughly mash with a fork. Add the cooled potato to a large mixing bowl along with the peas, garlic granules, chives, lemon zest and juice. Stir to roughly combine. Remove the cod fillets from the pan and discard the cooking liquor. Add the fish to the bowl with the potato and mix. Season with salt and pepper to taste.

Add half the beaten egg and 30g of the breadcrumbs to the bowl and combine. Divide the mixture into 6 in the bowl. Shape the mixture into 6 fishcakes and place them on a plate. Pop into the fridge for 30 minutes to firm up before cooking.

Add the remaining egg to a plate and remaining panko breadcrumbs to another plate. Dip each fishcake first into the egg and then into the panko breadcrumbs, getting a good coverage on each fishcake. Place into the air fryer basket and spray with low-calorie cooking spray.

Air-fry at 180°C for 20 minutes, turning the fishcakes over halfway through cooking, and spray the tops with more low-calorie cooking spray.

In a small bowl combine the mayonnaise, tartare sauce and lemon juice, mixing until smooth. Serve the fishcakes with the sauce.

FETA-STUFFED FALAFELS

🕐 **20 MINS**   🍲 **8–10 MINS**   ✕ **SERVES 4**

PER SERVING:
172 KCAL /15G CARBS

SPECIAL EQUIPMENT:
Food processor

FOR THE YOGHURT DRESSING
125g fat-free Greek yoghurt
½ tsp dried dill
1 tsp runny honey
juice of ½ lemon
sea salt and freshly ground
    black pepper

FOR THE FALAFELS
30g rolled porridge oats
40g spinach
a good handful of fresh
    coriander
a good handful of fresh parsley
1 small onion, peeled and
    roughly chopped
3 garlic cloves, peeled
1 x 400g tin chickpeas,
    drained and rinsed
grated zest of ½ lemon
2 tsp ground cumin
100g reduced-fat feta cheese,
    cut into 12 even-sized pieces
low-calorie cooking spray

TO ACCOMPANY
75g mixed salad (+15 kcal per
    serving) and a wholemeal
    pitta bread (+184 kcal per
    serving)

Just in case these little chickpea bites weren't tasty enough already, we've ramped up the flavour by hiding creamy feta cheese in the centre of each one. It might be true that traditional deep-fried falafel recipes work better with dried chickpeas, but the beauty of your air fryer is that you'll get crispy golden bites using the convenient tinned version. That means less time soaking chickpeas, and more time enjoying your herby homemade falafels, with that salty feta surprise in the middle!

Everyday Light

Mix the yoghurt, dill, honey and lemon juice together in a bowl. Stir in a little water to thin the yoghurt down to a drizzling consistency. Taste and season with a little salt and pepper, if required. Cover and refrigerate until ready to serve.

Place the oats in a food processor and blitz to a coarse flour. Put into a bowl and set to one side.

Now add the spinach to the food processor, followed by the fresh herbs, onion, garlic, chickpeas, lemon zest and cumin. Add the blitzed oats and season with salt and pepper. Blitz in several pulses, scraping down the sides when necessary, until the mix is finely ground and starting to come together.

Scrape out into a bowl and divide into 12 equal portions. Roll each portion of falafel mix into a ball and flatten slightly in your hand. Press a piece of feta into the middle, wrap the falafel mix around the feta so it is fully enclosed, and shape into a ball.

Add the falafels to the air fryer basket and spray with low-calorie cooking spray. Air-fry at 200°C for 6 minutes, then flip with tongs and cook for a further 3–4 minutes, until crisp and golden on the outside.

You can freeze the falafel at this point; place them in airtight, freezerproof containers once cold. Defrost overnight in the fridge and reheat in the air fryer at 180°C for around 5 minutes, or until piping hot throughout.

Serve with plenty of mixed salad, a drizzle of yoghurt dressing and some warm wholemeal pitta.

FAKEAWAYS

USE DF
YOGHURT

USE GF PUFF PASTRY

CURRY PUFFS

🕐 **10 MINS**   🍲 **23 MINS**   ✕ **SERVES 6**

PER PUFF:
258 KCAL / 33G CARBS

SPECIAL EQUIPMENT:
Frying pan with lid

low-calorie cooking spray
1 small potato, peeled and
 finely diced
½ carrot, peeled and finely
 diced
½ onion, peeled and finely diced
2 garlic cloves, peeled and
 minced
2 tsp curry powder, mild or hot
 depending on preference
100ml vegetable stock
 (1 vegetable stock cube
 dissolved in 100ml boiling
 water)
1 tbsp fat-free Greek yoghurt
1 tbsp/25g frozen peas
½ tsp honey
320g packet of ready-rolled
 light puff pastry
sea salt and freshly ground
 black pepper

These veggie-friendly puff-pastry parcels are great as a curry night side dish or as a mess-free lunchbox snack. From parties to picnics, there's always room on the buffet table for our crunchy Curry Puffs. So simple to rustle up, they're even quicker to make if you already have some leftover curry to use. If not, our mildly spiced vegetable filling will come together in no time, ready to bundle inside ready-rolled light puff pastry.

Weekly Indulgence

Spray a frying pan with low-calorie cooking spray. Add the potato, carrot, onion, garlic and curry powder to the pan. Cook over a medium–high heat for 3 minutes to cook the spices and colour the vegetables.

Add the vegetable stock to the frying pan and give it a stir. Reduce the heat to medium and place the lid on the pan. Cook for another 10 minutes, until the vegetables are soft and cooked through. The liquid should have reduced – if not, cook without the lid until the mix is almost dry.

Take the pan off the heat and stir in the yoghurt, peas and honey until combined. Season with salt and pepper to taste.

Cut the pastry into 6 equal pieces. The pieces will be almost square. Split the vegetable mixture across the 6 pieces. Place it on one side so you can fold the pastry diagonally to make triangular parcels. press the edges together and crimp with a fork to secure. Spray the triangles with low-calorie cooking spray. Place into the air fryer basket. You will need to leave a little space between the parcels to allow for the pastry to expand. You may need to do this in batches, depending on the size of your air fryer.

Air-fry at 180°C for 10 minutes, turning halfway through, until the curry puffs are golden brown. Once cooked, either serve straight away or place on a wire rack so they stay crispy.

For freezing and reheating guidelines see page 17.

TIP:

You could use leftover curry for the filling of these to turn it into a lunch-box-friendly meal.

CRISPY CHILLI BEEF

🕐 **10 MINS** 🍲 **15 MINS** ✕ **SERVES 4**

PER SERVING:
279 KCAL /19G CARBS

SPECIAL EQUIPMENT:
Large frying pan or wok

1 medium egg, beaten
1½ tbsp self-raising flour
500g lean rump steak, cut into
   thin strips
low-calorie cooking spray
1 red pepper, deseeded and
   sliced
1 carrot, peeled and cut into
   thin strips
½ onion, peeled and sliced
5 spring onions, trimmed and
   sliced
½ red chilli, chopped, or ½ tsp
   dried chilli flakes
2 garlic cloves, peeled and
   finely chopped
1.5cm (¾in) piece of root ginger,
   peeled and finely chopped
juice of 1 lime
2 tsp granulated sweetener
6 tbsp soy sauce
3 tbsp rice vinegar
1 tsp honey
2 drops Frank's Buffalo Wings
   Hot Sauce or other hot sauce
100ml beef stock (½ beef stock
   cube dissolved in 100ml
   boiling water)
sea salt and freshly ground
   black pepper

TO ACCOMPANY
125g cooked basmati rice
   (+173 kcal per serving)

TIP:

Use white granulated sweetener
that has the same weight, texture
and sweetness as sugar.

The ingredients list for this Crispy Chilli Beef is on the longer side but, trust us, once you've tried a crisped-up piece of tender beef, there'll be no regrets! You won't find any hidden nasties or lashings of oil here; we've used trusty herbs and spices to recreate takeaway-style flavours for fewer calories. Remember to hold off on adding your beef strips to the pan until you're ready to serve with basmati rice or noodles – they'll stay crispy for longer!

Weekly Indulgence —————————————

Add the beaten egg to a plate and the flour to a separate plate. Season the strips of beef with salt and pepper and dip each one into the beaten egg, then quickly drag it through the flour to give a light coating.

Spray the air fryer basket with low-calorie cooking spray and place the coated beef inside. Air-fry at 200°C for 15 minutes, giving the basket a shake regularly to ensure even cooking.

While the beef is cooking, spray a wok or frying pan with some low-calorie cooking spray. Then, over a medium–high heat, fry the pepper, carrot, onion, spring onions, chilli, garlic and ginger. Cook for 5 minutes, then add the lime juice, granulated sweetener, soy sauce, rice vinegar and honey. Stir, then add a couple of drops of hot sauce and the beef stock. Allow to cook for 1–5 minutes, depending how thick you would like the sauce.

When the beef is cooked and crispy, add it to the sauce in the frying pan and stir well. Serve with basmati rice or an accompaniment of your choice.

USE DF
YOGHURT

CHICKEN TIKKA MASALA

🕐 **20 MINS + 2 HOURS MARINATING**   🍲 **45 MINS**   ✕ **SERVES 4**

PER SERVING:
248 KCAL /16G CARBS

SPECIAL EQUIPMENT:
Food processor or blender, stick blender

FOR THE SPICE MIX
1 tsp ground paprika
1 tsp ground coriander
1 tsp ground cumin
2 tsp garam masala
1 tsp garlic granules
½ tsp mild chilli powder

FOR THE CHICKEN TIKKA
50g fat-free Greek yoghurt
1 tbsp fresh lemon juice
a few drops of red food
   colouring (optional)
500g skinless, boneless chicken
   breasts, cut into even-sized
   2.5cm (1in) cubes

FOR THE SAUCE
1 onion, peeled and roughly
   chopped
4 garlic cloves, peeled
3cm (1¼in) piece of root
   ginger, peeled
1 red chilli, deseeded (or leave
   the seeds in for extra spice)
low-calorie cooking spray
1 tsp salt
1 x 400g tin chopped tomatoes
500ml plant-based coconut drink
juice of ½ lemon
1 tbsp mango chutney
50g fat-free Greek yoghurt
a good handful of fresh
   coriander leaves, chopped

TO ACCOMPANY
125g cooked basmati rice
   (+173 kcal per serving)

No Pinch of Nom cookbook is complete without one of our oh-so-popular fakeaway curries! Air fryers are ideal for recreating the mouthwatering charred flavours that you usually only get from cooking in a tandoori oven – which is what makes this Chicken Tikka Masala taste as good as a takeaway. The spice-coated chicken pieces cook nice and quickly, keeping them juicy inside, but crisp on the outside. By the time they're ready to be stirred into the mild, creamy sauce, you won't want to wait another minute to dig in!

Weekly Indulgence ─────────────

Combine the spices for the spice mix in a bowl. In a large non-metallic bowl, make the tikka marinade by mixing the Greek yoghurt with 1 tablespoon of the spice mix. Add the lemon juice and a few drops of red food colouring, if using. Stir well and add the diced chicken, mixing until all the pieces are well coated in the marinade. Cover and place in the fridge to marinate for at least 2 hours, or overnight.

To make the sauce, place the onion, garlic, ginger and chilli in a food processor or blender and blitz to a paste. Set a non-stick pan over a medium–low heat. Spray well with low-calorie cooking spray. When hot, add the blended paste and the salt, and fry gently for 10 minutes, until it is dry and a golden colour. Add the remaining spice mix to the paste and cook for a minute or two until fragrant. Stir in the tomatoes and coconut drink and bring to the boil. Reduce the heat to a simmer, cover and cook for 30 minutes.

About 5 minutes before the end of the cooking time, spray your air fryer basket with low-calorie cooking spray and add the marinated chicken. Spritz the top with low-calorie cooking spray and air-fry for 8–10 minutes at 200°C, turning halfway through. You may need to do this in batches, depending on the size of your air fryer.

While the chicken tikka cooks, remove the sauce from the heat, stir in the lemon juice and mango chutney, and, using a stick blender, carefully blitz until smooth. Stir in the yoghurt and chopped coriander. Add the cooked chicken pieces and stir to coat, then serve with basmati rice.

For freezing and reheating guidelines see page 17.

FAKEAWAYS

CHICKEN SOUVLAKI
and TZATZIKI

🕐 **10 MINS+ 1 HOUR MARINATING**　　🍲 **25 MINS**　　✕ **SERVES 4**

PER SERVING:
220 KCAL /5.2G CARBS

SPECIAL EQUIPMENT:
8 skewers (wooden or metal) to fit your air fryer

FOR THE SOUVLAKI
4 skinless and boneless chicken breasts (170g each), cut into even-sized 2.5cm (1in) chunks
juice of 1 lemon
1 tbsp dried oregano
1 tbsp paprika
1 tsp dried thyme
½ tsp ground cumin
½ tsp garlic granules
½ tsp salt
pinch of freshly ground black pepper
pinch of cayenne pepper
low-calorie cooking spray

FOR THE TZATZIKI
160g fat-free natural yoghurt
2 tsp lemon juice
2 tsp garlic granules
1 tsp mint sauce
sea salt and freshly ground black pepper

TO ACCOMPANY
low-calorie tortilla wrap (+105 kcal per wrap) and 75g mixed salad (optional, +15 kcal per serving)

Anyone who loves a takeaway kebab can't help but adore this Chicken Souvlaki recipe. We've marinated chicken chunks in a homemade Mediterranean-style blend of citrus and spices, and threaded them onto skewers to air-fry. The results are unbelievably flavourful and tender, making it the perfect midweek treat. It's all cooked in just 25 minutes, including our lower-calorie Tzatziki (we've swirled zingy lemon juice together with mint sauce and creamy fat-free yoghurt).

Everyday Light

Add the chunks of chicken to a bowl. Add the lemon juice and mix until well coated. Add the rest of the Souvlaki chicken ingredients, except the low-calorie cooking spray, to the bowl and mix well until coated. Cover the bowl and place in the fridge for at least 1 hour.

If using wooden skewers for the chicken, put them into water to soak while the chicken marinates.

Slide your chicken pieces onto the skewers, dividing them evenly among 4, then spray them with low-calorie cooking spray. Place the skewers into the air fryer and air-fry at 180°C for 25 minutes, turning halfway.

While the chicken is cooking, place all the Tzatziki ingredients in a bowl and mix well. Season to taste.

Check the chicken is cooked and white throughout, then serve on a tortilla wrap with the Tzatziki and some mixed salad, if you like.

For freezing and reheating guidelines see page 17.

CHICKEN IN ORANGE

🕐 **15 MINS**　🍲 **12 MINS**　✕ **SERVES 4**

PER SERVING:
269 KCAL /27G CARBS

500g skinless, boneless chicken
　breasts, cut into even-sized,
　2.5cm (1in) chunks
1 tsp toasted sesame oil
2 tsp light soy sauce
½ tsp garlic granules
1 heaped tbsp cornflour
low-calorie cooking spray
1 tsp sesame seeds, to garnish

FOR THE SAUCE
3 spring onions, trimmed and
　thinly sliced
1 tsp finely grated orange zest
juice of 2 oranges (around
　200ml, but no need to be
　exact)
150ml water
3 tbsp light soy sauce
1 tbsp rice vinegar
2cm (¾in) piece of root ginger,
　peeled and finely grated
2 garlic cloves, peeled and
　crushed
2 tbsp runny honey
4 tsp cornflour, mixed to a slurry
　with 4 tsp cold water
1 tsp granulated sweetener
　(optional)

TO ACCOMPANY
125g cooked basmati rice
　(+173 kcal per serving)

Meet the new, improved version of one of our favourite fakeaways! Our classic Chicken in Orange recipe has been reinvented for your air fryer. We reckon you'll agree this ramps up the flavours and brings a new freshness to the finished dish. Plus, you can't beat the way the chicken crisps up in the air fryer, ready to be smothered in that sticky-sweet sauce.

Weekly Indulgence

Place the chicken in a bowl and pour over the sesame oil and soy sauce. Sprinkle over the garlic granules and mix well to evenly coat the chicken. Cover and refrigerate for 10 minutes to allow the flavours to mingle (you can use this time to prepare your sauce ingredients).

Put the cornflour on a plate. Add the chicken and toss around, making sure each piece of chicken is well coated. The soy sauce and sesame oil marinade will combine with the cornflour to form a light, batter-like coating on the chicken.

Spray the air fryer basket with low-calorie cooking spray. Add the chicken, making sure the pieces are not overlapping (cook in 2 batches if you need to). Air-fry at 200°C for 10–12 minutes, until the chicken is cooked through and the coating has become golden and crisp on the edges.

While the chicken cooks, separate the white parts of the spring onions from the green (reserve these for garnishing) and place in a small saucepan, along with the orange zest, orange juice, water, soy sauce, rice vinegar, ginger, garlic and honey. Place on the hob over a high heat and bring to the boil. Reduce the heat to a simmer and cook for 2 minutes. Stir in the cornflour slurry and allow to bubble away for 3–4 minutes, until the sauce is glossy and thick enough to coat the chicken. Taste and add some granulated sweetener if you need to (this will depend on the sweetness of your oranges and your own personal taste).

Serve the chicken with the sauce drizzled over the top, garnished with the green spring onions and sesame seeds, alongside some basmati rice.

FAKEAWAYS

FREEZE ME

DAIRY FREE

USE DF CHEESE

GLUTEN FREE

USE GF WRAP

CHICKEN *and* SWEETCORN PIZZA CALZONE

🕐 **5 MINS**   🍲 **7 MINS**   ✕ **SERVES 1**

PER SERVING:
479 KCAL /31G CARBS

1 low-calorie tortilla wrap
1 tbsp passata
pinch of dried basil (optional)
pinch of garlic granules
  (optional)
½ skinless chicken breast,
  cooked and diced
2 tbsp drained tinned
  sweetcorn
¼ red pepper, deseeded
  and diced
40g reduced-fat Cheddar,
  finely grated
1 egg, beaten
low-calorie cooking spray

TO ACCOMPANY *(optional)*
75g mixed salad
  (+15 kcal per serving)

You might not expect to find calzone on a slimming-friendly meal plan, but we've brought the calories down using a surprise ingredient . . . low-calorie tortilla wraps! Once they're baked in the air fryer, they act as the perfect crispy shell to hold our scrumptious chicken and sweetcorn pizza-inspired filling. The trick is to not overfill them – while they're delicious regardless, you don't want them exploding before you've had a chance to take your first bite!

Weekly Indulgence ⎯⎯⎯⎯⎯⎯⎯

Take the wrap and spread the passata over half of it, being careful not to get any too close to the edge. If using basil and garlic, sprinkle these over the passata.

Place the chicken, sweetcorn, pepper and cheese on top of the passata (again, be careful not to get any too close to the edge). Try not to overfill as this will make it difficult to seal! Brush all around the edges of the wrap with beaten egg.

Fold the wrap in half and press down around the edge, crimping with the back of a fork. Brush the top of the calzone with beaten egg.

Place into the air fryer basket and spray with low-calorie cooking spray. Air-fry at 200°C for 7 minutes, until golden brown and piping hot throughout.

For freezing and reheating guidelines see page 17.

FAKEAWAYS

DAIRY FREE

GLUTEN FREE

USE GF
SOY SAUCE

CHICKEN *and* PINEAPPLE SKEWERS

🕐 **20 MINS*** 🍲 **10–12 MINS** ✕ **SERVES 4**

*+ 30 MINS MARINATING, 20 MINS SOAKING

PER SERVING:
211 KCAL /16G CARBS

SPECIAL EQUIPMENT:
8 bamboo skewers,
pastry brush

FOR THE MARINADE
2 tbsp tomato ketchup
½ tsp garlic granules
½ tsp ground ginger
1 tsp dark soy sauce
1 tsp Henderson's relish
1 tbsp runny honey
2 tbsp pineapple juice

FOR THE SKEWERS
500g skinless, boneless
   chicken breasts, cut into
   evenly sized 2cm (¾in) dice
1 red or orange pepper,
   deseeded and cut into
   2cm (¾in) dice
4 tinned pineapple rings in
   juice, drained and each cut
   into 6 (reserve 2 tbsp of juice
   for the marinade)
low-calorie cooking spray
lime wedges, to serve

TO ACCOMPANY
75g mixed salad
   (+15 kcal per serving)

TIP:

Make sure you use tinned (not
fresh) pineapple and juice for
this recipe. There is an enzyme
present in fresh pineapple that
will cause the chicken to become
soft and mushy if left to marinate.

These zesty pineapple skewers take next to no effort to put
together with the help of your trusty air fryer! The perfect
blend of sweet and savoury, we've threaded together juicy
pineapple chunks, tender chicken pieces and colourful
chopped peppers. This recipe's punchy magic comes from
the surprisingly simple homemade marinade, made with
store-cupboard staples, a dash of Henderson's relish and
fruity pineapple juice. The results are mouthwateringly
good . . . and only 214 calories per person for 2 skewers!

Everyday Light ───────────────────────

Mix the marinade ingredients together in a small bowl.

Place the chicken in a large non-metallic bowl. Add the
marinade but reserve 2 tablespoons for basting later. Mix
well to thoroughly coat the chicken, cover, and allow to
marinate in the fridge for at least 30 minutes (you can leave
for longer, or even overnight if you wish).

Soak the bamboo skewers in water for 20 minutes before
starting to cook. This will prevent them burning in the air fryer.

To assemble, pat the bamboo skewers dry, then thread
on a piece of pepper, a piece of chicken and a piece of
pineapple. Repeat so you have 3 pieces of pepper, chicken
and pineapple, alternating on each skewer.

Place the skewers in the air fryer basket and spritz with
a little low-calorie cooking spray. Air-fry at 180°C for
5 minutes, then carefully turn the skewers over. You may
need to do this in batches, depending on the size of your
air fryer. Using a pastry brush, baste the skewers with the
reserved marinade and cook for another 5–7 minutes, until
the chicken is thoroughly cooked.

Serve 2 skewers per portion, with a wedge of lime and
some mixed salad.

FAKEAWAYS

BAKES *and* ROASTS

CRISPY LEMON *and* PARMESAN CHICKEN

🕐 **15 MINS + 1 HOUR MARINATING**   🍳 **12–14 MINS**   ✕ **SERVES 4**

PER SERVING:
206 KCAL / 6.5G CARBS

SPECIAL EQUIPMENT:
Food processor

FOR THE MARINADE
50g fat-free natural yoghurt
1 tsp garlic granules
finely grated zest of 1 lemon
2 tsp lemon juice
freshly ground black pepper

FOR THE CHICKEN
4 large skinless, boneless
   chicken thighs, approx.
   125g each
1 thick slice wholemeal
   bread (approx. 45g),
   blitzed into crumbs
25g Parmesan cheese,
   finely grated
low-calorie cooking spray
lemon wedges, to serve

TO ACCOMPANY
75g mixed salad
   (+15 kcal per serving)

TIP:

The yoghurt marinade will
help flavour and tenderize the
chicken thighs, and also helps
the breadcrumbs stick. Don't be
tempted to use more than the
recipe states, as this can make
the coating soggy.

Juicy, tasty and great value for money, we love thinking
up new ways to cook chicken thighs! You can't go wrong
with the vibrant flavour combo of lemon and Parmesan,
especially when you throw some crispy breadcrumbs into
the mix. Our yoghurt-based marinade is super important
for adding flavour and tenderizing the meat, so make sure
you plan ahead to let the chicken marinate for at least
an hour. When you're ready for dinner, it'll only take
12–14 minutes for your air fryer to do its thing!

Everyday Light ─────────────────────

Mix the yoghurt, garlic granules, lemon zest and juice and
pepper together in a non-metallic bowl.

Trim the chicken thighs of any fat, open up and flatten
slightly with the heel of your hand. They will naturally open
up into an escalope shape.

Add them to the bowl and rub over the marinade, ensuring
they are well covered. There should only be a light covering
of marinade. Cover and marinate in the fridge for at least
1 hour, but you can prep in the morning for cooking later if
you want.

After marinating, mix the breadcrumbs and grated
Parmesan together on a plate. Take each thigh and coat
with the breadcrumb mix. The yoghurt marinade will help
the breadcrumbs stick to the thighs.

Spray the air fryer basket with low-calorie cooking spray
and place in the coated thighs, leaving enough space in
between for air to circulate. Spritz the tops with low-calorie
cooking spray and air-fry at 200°C for 12–14 minutes,
flipping over halfway through.

When cooked, the coating should be crisp and golden
and there should be no pink remaining. Serve with lemon
wedges for squeezing and a mixed salad. You can add
some extra parmesan shavings to the saled if you like but
don't forget to adjust the calories accordingly.

CREAMY PESTO SALMON

⏱ **10 MINS**   🍲 **10 MINS**   ✕ **SERVES 2**

PER SERVING:
345 KCAL /3.6G CARBS

50g reduced-fat cream cheese
1 tbsp green pesto
1 tsp finely grated lemon zest
2 x 110g skinless salmon fillets
2 tbsp panko breadcrumbs
low-calorie cooking spray
sea salt and freshly ground
   black pepper

TO ACCOMPANY
80g steamed vegetables (+38
   kcal per serving) and 120g
   boiled new potatoes (+90 kcal
   per serving)

Pencil this in for your next Friday fish supper! We've stuffed juicy salmon fillets with a simple mixture of cream cheese and pesto, with a hint of zingy lemon zest to liven up the flavours. Before baking to flaky perfection in the air fryer, each fillet gets topped with a lemony, salt-and-pepper-seasoned panko breadcrumb crust, which crisps up a treat as they cook. All you need to add is a portion of steamed veggies and new potatoes for an easy dinner that's ready in a flash.

Weekly Indulgence

Mix the cream cheese with the pesto, half of the lemon zest and a pinch of black pepper.

Make a pocket in your salmon fillets. Using a small, sharp knife, make a cut, lengthways, down the middle of the thickest part of the salmon fillet. Start 1–2cm (½–¾in) from the top and stop cutting as the salmon fillet becomes thinner. Make sure you don't cut right through the salmon. Fill these pockets with the cream cheese and pesto mix and spread any remaining mix over the top of the fillet. If you are using tail-end salmon fillets, these won't be thick enough to make a pocket, so just spread the pesto cream cheese over the top.

In a small bowl, mix the breadcrumbs with the remaining lemon zest, season with salt and pepper, then spray with low-calorie cooking spray.

Press the breadcrumbs onto the top of the salmon to form a crust. Carefully place into the air fryer basket and air-fry at 200°C for 10 minutes, until the salmon is cooked through and the breadcrumbs are crisp and golden. Serve with steamed vegetables and boiled new potatoes.

WHOLE CHICKEN

 10 MINS    **1 HOUR + 10 MINS RESTING**   ✕ **SERVES 6**

PER SERVING:
278 KCAL /1.6G CARBS

6 garlic cloves, peeled
small bunch of fresh rosemary
medium chicken, approx. 1.5kg
1 lemon, cut in half
low-calorie cooking spray
sea salt and freshly ground
  black pepper

TO ACCOMPANY *(optional)*
80g steamed green vegetables
  (+38 kcal per serving), Roast
  Potatoes (see page 126)
  (+315 kcal per serving)

Once you've cooked a whole chicken in your air fryer, you'll probably never want to cook it any other way. Roasted to perfection in an hour, it stays unbelievably succulent with very little effort needed. Using just a few simple ingredients, we've infused our chicken with gentle, subtle flavours that keep it nice and versatile. The aromatic hint of garlic, lemon and rosemary means you can pair the cooked chicken with salad, use it in sandwiches or add all the trimmings to turn it into your best ever Sunday roast.

Everyday Light ———————————————

Use the back of a knife to give the garlic and rosemary a good bash to release their flavours. Pop both inside the cavity of the chicken, along with the lemon halves.

Spray the top of the chicken with low-calorie cooking spray and season well with salt and pepper. Place breast-side down in the air fryer basket. This will keep the breast moist as the cooking juices are released.

Air-fry at 200°C for 40 minutes, then carefully turn the chicken over and cook for another 20 minutes to crisp up the breast. Cut into the thickest part of the chicken to check it is thoroughly cooked. The juices should run clear and there should be no pink remaining. Allow to rest for 5–10 minutes before carving.

Any leftovers can be removed from the bone, portioned into freezerproof containers and frozen (see page 17 for further guidelines).

BAKES AND ROASTS

SAUSAGE TRAYBAKE

⏱ **15 MINS**   🍲 **30 MINS**   ✕ **SERVES 2**

DAIRY FREE

GLUTEN FREE
USE GF SAUSAGES

PER SERVING:
359 KCAL /53G CARBS

SPECIAL EQUIPMENT:
Air fryer liner (optional)

250g new potatoes, halved
   (or cut into wedges if large)
2 medium carrots, peeled and
   cut into chunks, about the
   same size as the potatoes
4 reduced-fat pork sausages
1 medium red onion, peeled
   and cut into wedges
½ eating apple, cored and
   sliced
low-calorie cooking spray
1 tbsp honey
1 tbsp wholegrain mustard
½ tsp garlic granules
50ml apple juice
a few sprigs of fresh thyme
sea salt and freshly ground
   black pepper

We've given one of our most popular midweek meals an air fryer makeover, and it works like a gem! Budget-friendly bangers don't come tastier than this simple traybake, with hearty potatoes, carrots and a sticky-sweet honey and mustard glaze. Pork and apple go together like a dream come true, so we've even thrown a few apple slices into the air fryer, to keep things fruity. Best of all, everything cooks so much faster than the oven version of this recipe, but it tastes just as delicious as you remember!

Everyday Light ────────────────

Place the potatoes and carrots in a saucepan, cover with cold water and bring to the boil over a medium heat. Cook for 5 minutes, until you can pierce the veg with a fork, then drain well.

Remove the basket from your air fryer or, if you are unable, add an air fryer liner. Place the sausages, onion and apple into the air fryer with the potatoes and carrots. Spray well with low-calorie cooking spray, season with a little salt and pepper and mix to coat the vegetables evenly. Air-fry at 190°C for 15 minutes, stirring halfway to ensure even cooking.

In a small bowl, mix the honey, mustard, garlic granules and apple juice. Pour over the sausages and vegetables. Add some thyme sprigs and cook for a further 10 minutes, until the sausages are cooked and the vegetables are browned.

Divide between two plates and serve at once!

FAN FAVOURITE

'Great comfort food
on a cosy day'
Michelle Theobald

VEGGIE

USE VEGETARIAN
SAUSAGES, CUT
INTO SLICES AND
VEGETARIAN STOCK
CUBES

**FREEZE
ME**

**BATCH
COOK**

SAUSAGE PASTA BAKE

🕐 **20 MINS** 🍲 **30 MINS** ✕ **SERVES 4**

PER SERVING:
494 KCAL /56G CARBS

SPECIAL EQUIPMENT:
**18cm (7in) square deep cake tin
or silicone mould (optional)**

400g pack of reduced-fat pork
   sausages
200g dried pasta shapes (we
   used macaroni)
1 red onion, peeled and cut into
   1cm (½in) dice
1 pepper (any colour), deseeded
   and cut into 1cm (½in) dice
1 small courgette, cut into 1cm
   (½in) dice
1 x 400g tin chopped tomatoes
2 tsp dried mixed Italian herbs
2 tsp garlic granules
1 tbsp balsamic vinegar
2 tbsp tomato puree
100ml chicken stock (1 chicken
   stock cube dissolved in 100ml
   boiling water)
50g reduced-fat mature
   Cheddar, finely grated
125g reduced-fat mozzarella,
   grated

TIPS:

Make sure the pasta is still
hot when you add it to the air
fryer, to cut down on air fryer
cooking time.

We remove the skins from our
sausages. This isn't essential,
but the skin on reduced-fat
sausages can sometimes be a
little tough. If you choose not
to do this, simply slice each
sausage into 4 or 5 pieces and
follow the instructions.

A pasta bake for dinner is always a tasty way to guarantee
empty plates all round. This family-friendly recipe is no
exception, combining reduced-fat pork sausages and
fresh veggies with filling pasta, underneath a melty, cheesy
topping. The whole thing is dished up straight from the air
fryer in just half an hour, leaving behind minimal pots and
pans to clean. If you ask us, that deserves a spot on your
meal plan this week!

Weekly Indulgence ─────────────

Depending on your style of air fryer, either remove the basket
and cook directly in the air fryer drawer or use a 18cm (7in)
square deep cake tin or dish that fits into your air fryer.

Squeeze the sausage meat out of the skins and shape into
rough balls. Place in the bottom of the air fryer drawer or tin.
Don't worry if they stick together. Air-fry at 200°C for 5 minutes.

Meanwhile, add the pasta to a pan of boiling salted water
and cook for around 10 minutes, until 'al dente'.

Add the onion, pepper and courgette to the sausage in
the air fryer, stir well, breaking up any sausage bits that
have stuck together. Cook for a further 8 minutes, stirring
halfway through.

Mix together the tomatoes, herbs, garlic granules, balsamic
vinegar, tomato puree and stock. Drain the pasta. When the
sausages and vegetables have finished cooking, stir in the
tomato sauce and drained pasta.

Set the air fryer temperature to 180°C and air-fry for
12 minutes, stirring halfway through.

Sprinkle over the Cheddar and mozzarella, increase the
temperature to 200°C and air-fry for another 5 minutes,
until the cheese is bubbling and golden. Serve.

To freeze, cool quickly and freeze in individual portions as
soon as possible after cooking. Defrost overnight in the
fridge, then reheat, loosely covered, in the microwave for
3–4 minutes, stirring halfway through, until piping hot. You
may need to add a splash of water.

BAKES AND ROASTS

USE GF FLOUR

COSY PIGS IN THE HOLE

🕐 **10 MINS**　📦 **30 MINS**　✕ **SERVES 2**

PER SERVING:
411 KCAL /31G CARBS

SPECIAL EQUIPMENT:
**Metal tin or disposable foil tray,
no bigger than 22cm x 16cm
(8½ x 6in)**

FOR THE PIGS IN BLANKETS
4 reduced-fat pork chipolatas,
　halved
4 bacon medallions, halved
　lengthways
low-calorie cooking spray

**FOR THE YORKSHIRE
PUDDING BATTER**

60g plain flour
140ml semi-skimmed milk
2 medium eggs
sea salt and freshly ground
　black pepper

TO ACCOMPANY
80g steamed vegetables
　(+38 kcal per serving)

Plain old Toad in the Hole will be off the menu once you've tried little piggy chipolatas wrapped inside cosy, crispy bacon blankets. We've gone the whole hog by nestling them into a fluffy Yorkshire pudding, and covering them in a rich glug of red onion gravy. We like these piggies best with a side of steamed vegetables, but there's nothing to stop you bringing them all the way home with a hearty serving of creamy mashed potatoes. It's pure, slimming-friendly comfort food for chillier days!

Weekly Indulgence ──────────────

Wrap each halved chipolata with a halved bacon medallion to make eight pigs in blankets. Place seam-side down on a plate and leave in the fridge while you make the Yorkshire pudding batter.

Sift the flour into a medium mixing bowl and season with salt and pepper. Place the milk and eggs in a measuring jug and beat with a fork or whisk until well combined.

Make a well in the centre of the flour and pour in a little of the milk and egg mixture. Draw in a little of the flour and mix well. Continue adding the liquid a little at a time until you have a smooth batter. Pour the batter into a measuring jug.

Spray the tin or disposable foil tray with low-calorie cooking spray and add the sausages. Place in the air fryer and air-fry at 200°C for 7 minutes.

After 7 minutes, remove from the air fryer and quickly pour the batter around the pigs in blankets, up to the rim of the tin. Quickly return to the air fryer and air-fry for another 20 minutes until risen, crisp and golden brown.

Serve with steamed vegetables and, if you like, some gravy (remember to adjust the calories accordingly).

Can be frozen as soon as completely cooled. Freeze in freezerproof containers. Defrost thoroughly in the fridge. Reheat in the air fryer until crisp and piping hot.

BAKES AND ROASTS

VEGGIE

USE VEGETARIAN
CHICKEN
ALTERNATIVE
AND STOCK

FREEZE
ME

BATCH
COOK

GLUTEN
FREE

USE GF PASTA,
STOCK, AND
BREADCRUMBS

CHICKEN KYIV PASTA BAKE

🕐 **20 MINS**   🍲 **25 MINS**   ✕ **SERVES 4**

PER SERVING:
406 KCAL /48G CARBS

SPECIAL EQUIPMENT:
**18cm (7in) square deep cake tin
or silicone mould (optional)**

low-calorie cooking spray
300g skinless, boneless chicken
   breast, cut into small pieces
2 medium leeks, trimmed and
   thinly sliced
4 garlic cloves, peeled and
   crushed
200g dried pasta shapes
   (whichever you prefer)
1 chicken stock pot dissolved in
   150ml boiling water
½ tsp Dijon mustard
100g button mushrooms, sliced
165g reduced-fat cream cheese
2 medium slices wholemeal
   bread, blitzed into crumbs
20g mature Cheddar, finely
   grated
1 tsp dried parsley
sea salt and freshly ground
   black pepper

TO ACCOMPANY *(optional)*
75g mixed salad (+15 kcal per
   serving)

A Pinch of Nom website fave, we've reimagined the oven version of our Chicken Kyiv Pasta Bake to make it even easier and fuss free. Other than the pasta (which needs to be boiled on the hob) you can cook the whole thing in your air fryer, so there's less to wash up after dinner! Once you've combined the creamy, garlicky chicken sauce with the cooked pasta, you'll sprinkle cheesy breadcrumbs on the top to give you an ultra-crispy, toasty crust.

Weekly Indulgence

Depending on your style of air fryer, either cook directly in the drawer (after removing the basket) or in an 18cm (7in) square cake tin or silicone liner. Spray the drawer or tin with low-calorie cooking spray and add the chicken, leeks and garlic. Stir, then spritz the top with low-calorie cooking spray. Air-fry at 180°C for 8 minutes, stirring halfway through.

Cook the pasta in a pan of boiling salted water, according to the packet instructions.

Stir the hot stock and Dijon mustard into the chicken and leeks, add the mushrooms on top, but don't stir. Air-fry for 5 minutes, stir in the cream cheese, then taste and season with salt and pepper if needed. Cook for a further 5 minutes.

Mix the breadcrumbs, Cheddar and parsley together in a small bowl.

Drain the pasta and stir into the creamy chicken while it's still hot. Sprinkle over the breadcrumb mix, then air-fry for another 8–10 minutes, until the breadcrumbs are crispy and golden and have formed a toasty crust on top (check occasionally to make sure you don't overdo them). Serve with a mixed salad, if you like.

For freezing and reheating guidelines see page 17.

TIP:

Make sure the pasta is hot
when you stir it into the sauce.

BAKES AND ROASTS

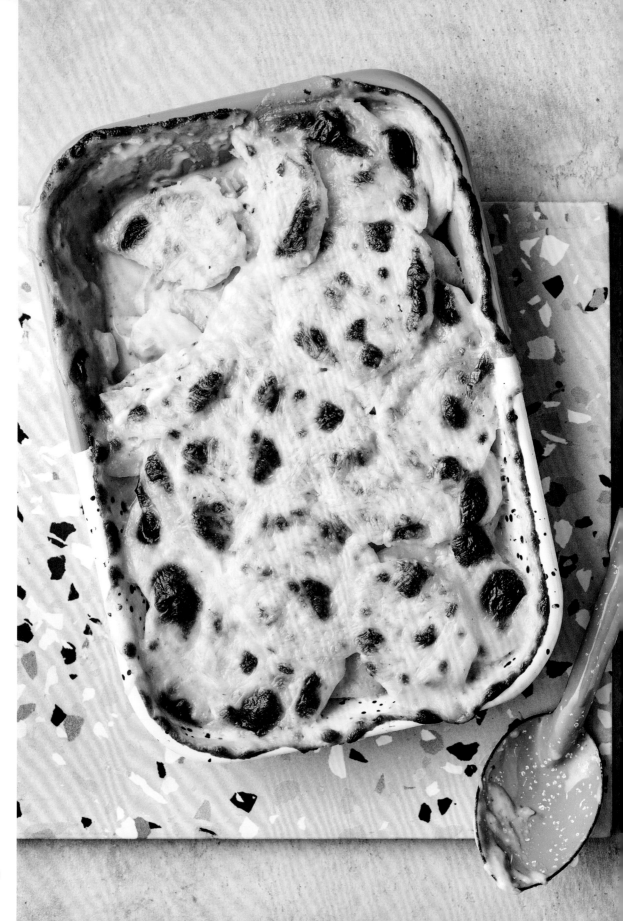

CHEESY POTATO GRATIN

🕐 **20 MINS** 🍲 **35 MINS** ✕ **SERVES 4**

PER SERVING:
236 KCAL / 32G CARBS

SPECIAL EQUIPMENT:
18cm (7in) square deep cake tin or silicone mould (optional)

500g potatoes, peeled
350ml skimmed milk
1 tsp garlic granules
1 tbsp cornflour, mixed to a slurry with 1 tbsp skimmed milk
50g reduced-fat spreadable cheese
20g Parmesan cheese, grated
50g reduced-fat mature Cheddar, finely grated
sea salt and freshly ground black pepper

We've used not one, not two, but THREE types of cheese to make sure these are the cheesiest potatoes to ever come out of an air fryer. Our easy gratin may look, sound and taste indulgent, yet it's only 236 calories per portion. Instead of heavy cream, our spuds are cooked in a velvety sauce made from skimmed milk, reduced-fat spreadable cheese and Parmesan. Topped with a sprinkling of Cheddar, it'll bubble away in the air fryer until the potatoes are tender and crispy round the edges.

Everyday Light

Thinly slice the potatoes, about 2mm thick, to ensure they cook evenly. Place in a bowl of cold water while you prepare the sauce.

Put the milk in a large saucepan, along with the garlic granules, over a medium heat and bring just about to the boil. Add the cornflour slurry and stir until thickened. Add the cheese spread and Parmesan and stir until melted and well combined. Taste and season with salt and pepper, if required.

Drain the potatoes and pat them dry with a tea towel. Add to the pan of cheese sauce and stir well. Cover and simmer for 10–15 minutes, stirring frequently until the potatoes are just cooked, but still holding their shape.

Depending on your style of air fryer, either pour directly into the drawer (after removing the basket) or pour into the cake tin or silicone mould. Sprinkle the grated Cheddar on top and air-fry at 180°C for 10–15 minutes until golden and bubbling.

Allow to stand for 5 minutes before serving.

TIP:

This makes a delicious side dish, and would be classed as Weekly Indulgence.

BAKES AND ROASTS

SALMON FISHCAKES

🕐 **15 MINS**   🍲 **30 MINS**   ✕ **SERVES 4**

PER SERVING:
250 KCAL /26G CARBS

SPECIAL EQUIPMENT:
potato masher
food processor

400g potatoes, peeled
  and cut into chunks
2 x 170g tins of skinless,
  boneless pink salmon, drained
75g frozen peas, cooked
  according to packet
  instructions
finely grated zest of 1 lemon
½ tsp dried dill
½ tsp dried parsley
1 tsp Dijon mustard
1 medium egg, beaten
60g wholemeal bread, blitzed
  into crumbs
low-calorie cooking spray
sea salt and freshly ground
  black pepper
½ lemon, cut into 4 wedges,
  to serve

TO ACCOMPANY
80g steamed vegetables
  (+38 kcal per serving)

You heard it here first, folks: air-fried fishcakes are a game changer! Who knew a couple of tins of salmon, some frozen peas and a slice or two of (almost) stale bread could be turned into such a dreamy dinner? We've added lots of lemon into the filling for these easy-peasy fishcakes, for a burst of zestiness that works beautifully with the sweetness of the peas. Coat each one in homemade breadcrumbs, then whack them in the air fryer until they're irresistibly crunchy on the outside.

Everyday Light ─────────────────

Cook the potatoes in a pan of boiling, salted water over a high heat for around 15 minutes, or until a knife slides easily through a potato. Drain well and return to the pan. Allow to air dry for 5 minutes, then mash well.

Place the mashed potato in a mixing bowl. Break the salmon into large flakes and add to the bowl along with the peas, lemon zest, dill, parsley and Dijon mustard. Taste and add salt and pepper if required. Shape the mixture into 4 equal-sized fishcakes.

Place the beaten egg and breadcrumbs onto separate plates. Carefully dip each fishcake into the egg, then lightly coat with the breadcrumbs.

Spray the air fryer basket with low-calorie cooking spray. Carefully place the fishcakes in, leaving a little space between each one. Spray the tops with low-calorie cooking spray and air-fry at 200°C for around 12 minutes, until crisp and golden brown.

To freeze, allow the fishcakes to cool and then wrap them individually. Defrost in the fridge and reheat in a moderate oven for around 10 minutes or in the air fryer for 5–8 minutes to keep them crisp. Handle carefully as they can become fragile when defrosted.

Serve with fresh lemon wedges and some steamed vegetables and, if you like, some low-fat mayonnaise (but adjust the calories accordingly).

CHEESE *and* BACON FILO TARTS

🕐 **10 MINS** 🍲 **20 MINS** ✕ **SERVES 4**

PER TART:
167 KCAL /8G CARBS

SPECIAL EQUIPMENT:
4 x 11cm (4 in) round foil pie dishes, approx. 3cm (1in) deep

4 bacon medallions
low-calorie cooking spray
3 medium eggs
60g reduced-fat cream cheese
20g baby spinach leaves, finely chopped, no stalks
2 spring onions, trimmed and finely chopped
30g reduced-fat Cheddar, finely grated
1/8 tsp mustard powder
pinch of freshly ground black pepper
2 sheets of filo pastry

Say hello to your new favourite, quick lunch recipe! Loaded up with cheese and bacon, you might not expect these tasty little tarts to be slimming-friendly, but they work out at just 167 calories each. To add the perfect crunch while keeping things light, we've used super-crispy filo pastry to make our golden tart cases. Each one gets filled with a dreamy, creamy cheese and egg mixture which firms up as it cooks. Serve these straight from the air fryer to make the most of the cheesy goodness.

Everyday Light

Cook the bacon in the air fryer at 200°C for 8–10 minutes. While the bacon is cooking, spray each pie dish with low-calorie cooking spray and rub it round the inside of the dish.

Using a whisk, mix the eggs and cream cheese together in a bowl and keep whisking until there are no lumps. Stir in the chopped spinach, chopped spring onions, half the grated cheese, the mustard powder and the pepper.

Chop the cooked bacon and stir into the egg mixture. Set aside for a minute while you clean the air fryer.

Working quickly so it doesn't dry out, take the 2 sheets of filo pastry and cut each sheet into 4 squares.

Place one square on top of another at an angle to make a star, then use those 2 squares to line a greased pie dish. Gently press the sides into the pie dish, and spray with a little low-calorie cooking spray. Do the same with the remaining 6 filo squares.

Stir the egg mixture and divide it equally between the 4 pastry-lined pie dishes. Place in the air fryer basket and air-fry at 160°C for 5 minutes. Sprinkle the remaining grated cheese equally over the tarts and cook for another 3–5 minutes at 160°C, until the centre has set, the cheese has melted and the filo is golden.

Carefully remove the tarts from the air fryer and allow to rest for a minute. Gently remove them from the foil trays and serve immediately.

BBQ MEATLOAF

🕐 **15 MINS**　🍲 **35 MINS + 5 MINS RESTING**　✕ **SERVES 4**

PER SERVING:
237 KCAL /14G CARBS

SPECIAL EQUIPMENT:
Pastry brush, food processor

low-calorie cooking spray
1 small onion, peeled and
　finely chopped
1 carrot, grated (no need to peel)
2 garlic cloves, peeled
　and crushed
500g 5%-fat beef mince
1 medium egg
1 tbsp Henderson's relish (or
　Worcestershire sauce)
1 tbsp BBQ seasoning
1 tsp dried oregano
1 tsp smoked sweet paprika
50g wholemeal bread,
　blitzed into crumbs
sea salt and freshly ground
　black pepper

FOR THE GLAZE
1 tsp BBQ seasoning
1 tbsp runny honey
½ tsp garlic granules
1 tbsp Henderson's relish (or
　Worcestershire sauce)
1 tbsp tomato puree
1 tsp balsamic vinegar

TO ACCOMPANY
250g mashed potato (+173 kcal
　per serving) and 80g steamed
　green vegetables (+38 kcal
　per serving)

TIP:

Remove the mince from the
fridge 20 minutes before
starting to cook, so it comes
to room temperature.

This is no ordinary meatloaf! A double whammy of lip-smacking BBQ flavour, we've packed smoky-sweet seasoning into our beef mince mixture, as well as adding it to the sticky glaze that's brushed on top as a final touch. Thanks to the veggies stashed inside, this meatloaf is nice and moist. From start to finish it takes less than an hour, then it's ready to be sliced up and served with mashed potatoes and extra vegetables on the side, with gravy too if you like (but remember to adjust the calories accordingly).

Everyday Light _____

Place a frying pan over a medium heat, spray with low-calorie cooking spray, add the onion, carrot and garlic and sauté for 5 minutes until soft.

Place the beef mince in a mixing bowl, along with the cooked carrot and onion. Beat the egg together in a bowl with the Henderson's relish, BBQ seasoning, oregano, paprika and a pinch of salt and pepper. Add to the mince and mix thoroughly (hands are best for this). Mix in the breadcrumbs and form into a loaf shape approximately 18 x 10cm (7 x 4in).

Cut a piece of baking parchment a little wider than the meatloaf, and about twice as long. Place the meatloaf in the centre and, using the baking parchment, lift into the air fryer basket. Air-fry at 180°C for 30 minutes.

Meanwhile, mix the glaze ingredients together in a bowl. After 30 minutes, open the air fryer and, using a pastry brush, spread the glaze evenly over the meatloaf. Return to the air fryer for another 5 minutes, until the glaze is sticky and the meatloaf is thoroughly cooked.

Carefully remove the meatloaf from the air fryer basket, using the baking parchment. Place on a plate and loosely cover with foil. Allow to rest for 5 minutes before serving. Cut into 12 slices and serve 3 slices per portion.

To freeze, cool quickly and wrap individual portions and place in an airtight container. To reheat, defrost overnight in the fridge, place on a microwavable plate, cover, then microwave for 2–3 minutes, turning halfway. Cook through until piping hot.

BAKES AND ROASTS

ROASTED PARMESAN SPROUTS

🕐 **5 MINS** 🍲 **20 MINS** ✕ **SERVES 4**

VEGGIE
USE VEGETARIAN HARD CHEESE

VEGAN
USE VEGAN PARMESAN ALTERNATIVE

LOW CARB

DAIRY FREE
USE DF PARMESAN ALTERNATIVE

GLUTEN FREE

PER SERVING:
99 KCAL /5.6G CARBS

500g Brussels sprouts, trimmed
low-calorie cooking spray
1 tsp garlic granules
½ tsp salt
30g Parmesan cheese, finely grated

Sprouts might not be the most popular veg out there, but we think we've done enough here to change anybody's mind! You only need five ingredients and five minutes to do the prep for these gorgeous Roasted Parmesan Sprouts. A gloriously green side dish, we've kept things nice and simple by making the most of a heavenly combination: punchy garlic and tangy Parmesan. Give them a good shake and sprinkle on the cheese a few minutes before serving, so it has time to turn irresistibly golden and crispy.

Everyday Light ─────────────────

Put the sprouts into the air fryer and spray with low-calorie cooking spray. Air-fry at 180°C for 10 minutes.

Tip the sprouts onto a plate. Now they will be soft enough to use the bottom of a glass to squish them so they flatten.

Spray again with low-calorie cooking spray and season with the garlic granules and salt and put back into the air fryer. Air-fry at 200°C for another 5 minutes.

Shake the basket and sprinkle the Parmesan on the top of the sprouts. Cook for a final 5 minutes, shaking halfway. Serve with a main of your choice.

BAKES AND ROASTS

VEGGIE

VEGAN

FREEZE ME

BATCH COOK

DAIRY FREE

GLUTEN FREE

ROAST POTATOES

🕐 **10 MINS**   🗑 **30 MINS + 5 MINS RESTING**   ✕ **SERVES 2**

PER SERVING:
315 KCAL /66G CARBS

2 large potatoes, peeled
low-calorie cooking spray
sea salt and freshly ground
  black pepper

OPTIONAL
½ tsp garlic granules
½ tsp dried rosemary

Stop right here – this is the recipe you're looking for! Even if you're new to the world of air fryers, everyone knows they're a game changer when it comes to spuds. There are plenty of opinions about how to make the perfect roastie, but this is the winner if you want crispy, golden potatoes without adding loads of fat or oil. For a crunchy outside and fluffy middle, follow our steps carefully, and don't be tempted to rush! You need to let the parboiled potatoes sit in the colander for five minutes before adding them into the air fryer. Trust us, it's worth the wait.

Special Occasion ──────────────

Dice the potatoes into pieces around 5cm (2in) in length and rinse with cold water. Place in a pan filled with cold water and add plenty of salt. Bring to the boil over a medium heat and let them cook for around 5 minutes, until they start to soften but are still firm.

Drain the potatoes in a colander and leave them there for 5 minutes. After 5 minutes, put them into a bowl, season with salt and pepper to taste, and, if using, add the garlic and rosemary. Give the bowl a shake to fluff up the edges of the potatoes.

Coat the potatoes with plenty of low-calorie cooking spray and tip them into the air fryer besket. Air-fry at 200°C for 25 minutes, making sure to shake the basket regularly. Once the potatoes are golden brown, crispy on the outside and soft and fluffy inside, they are ready to serve.

If you want to freeze these, as soon as they are cold, add to a container or bag that is suitable for freezing and place in the freezer. For reheating guidelines see page 17.

FAN FAVOURITE

'These always turn out lovely and crispy and they go perfectly with the PoN gravy recipe to make a really healthy roast dinner.'
Maxine Wooster

MAPLE-GLAZED GAMMON

🕐 **5 MINS**   🍲 **14 MINS**   ✕ **SERVES 2**

PER SERVING:
262 KCAL /14G CARBS

SPECIAL EQUIPMENT:
Pastry brush

4 tsp maple syrup
1½ tsp wholegrain mustard
1 tsp cider vinegar
2 x 150g gammon steaks,
  trimmed of fat
2 tinned peach halves,
  in juice, drained

TO ACCOMPANY
Mashed potatoes (+173 kcal per
  250g serving), 80g steamed
  green vegatables (+38 kcal
  per serving)

Back when we had a restaurant, gammon with peaches was one of our most popular dishes. We couldn't help but give it a whirl in the air fryer, and this is the result! The savoury saltiness of the gammon is more than a match for the sweet maple glaze, and topping it with half a soft, juicy peach is a lively twist on the traditional pineapple ring. Add some creamy mashed potato and steamed green veg on the side for a flavourful dining-out-style dinner that couldn't be easier to make.

Everyday Light

Mix the maple syrup, mustard and cider vinegar together in a small bowl.

Brush both sides of the gammon steaks with the glaze (saving some for basting) and place directly into the air fryer basket. Air-fry at 190°C for 4 minutes. After 4 minutes, baste the top with the glaze, flip, then baste the other side.

Continue cooking for a further 4 minutes. Baste the top with the glaze, place the peach halves on top and brush with any remaining glaze. Air-fry for another 4–6 minutes until the gammon is cooked and the glaze is deep golden and sticky.

Serve with mashed potato and some steamed green veg on the side.

TIP:

Gammon steaks come in many shapes and sizes. We used a 150g, half-horseshoe gammon steak, approximately 1cm (½in) thick. You may have to alter the cooking time or cook in batches to reflect the shape and thickness of your steak.

MAPLE-GLAZED CARROTS *and* PARSNIPS

🕐 **5 MINS**   🍲 **25 MINS**   ✕ **SERVES 4**

PER SERVING:
95 KCAL /16G CARBS

2 large carrots, peeled and
 cut into batons
2 large parsnips, peeled and
 cut into batons
low-calorie cooking spray
½ tsp garlic granules
1 tsp maple syrup
sea salt and freshly ground
 black pepper

Forget about waiting for Sunday to enjoy these sticky-sweet vegetables! Since they're ready in only half an hour, these dreamy roasted root veggies are our new favourite side dish for almost any meal. Adding just 95 calories to your plate per portion, you'll love the satisfying crunch and slight garlicky flavour they bring to dinnertime. Bookmark this page – you'll be turning to it time and time again!

Everyday Light ——————————————

In a bowl, coat the carrot and parsnip batons with low-calorie cooking spray. Season with salt and pepper and the garlic granules.

Add the vegetables to the air fryer basket and air-fry at 180°C for 20 minutes, shaking the basket halfway to ensure even cooking.

Give the basket a shake and drizzle over the maple syrup. Cook for a further 5 minutes and serve.

BAKES AND ROASTS

FREEZE ME

BATCH COOK

LOW CARB

DAIRY FREE

GLUTEN FREE

USE GF STOCK CUBE

KOFTE MEATBALL BAKE

🕐 **10 MINS**   🍲 **30 MINS**   ✕ **SERVES 4**

PER SERVING:
254 KCAL /7.2G CARBS

SPECIAL EQUIPMENT:
Silicone liner or foil tray approx.
22 x 16cm (8½ x 6in)

FOR THE MEATBALLS
500g 5%-fat beef mince
3 garlic cloves, peeled and diced
2cm (¾in) piece of root ginger, peeled and grated
½ tsp ground cumin
½ tsp ground allspice
2 tsp ground coriander
1 tsp ground cinnamon
1 tsp salt

FOR THE SAUCE
1 x 400g tin chopped tomatoes
½ beef stock cube, crumbled
1 tsp garlic powder
1 tsp onion granules
splash of Henderson's relish
1 tsp dried parsley
freshly ground black pepper

TO ACCOMPANY
125g cooked basmati rice
   (+173 kcal per serving)

These meatballs, with a Turkish-inspired twist, are batch-cookable, slimming-friendly and utterly delicious. By rolling our meatball mixture from scratch, we've cut down the calories and ramped up the flavour, using a blend of low-fat mince and an easy selection of aromatic spices. Your air fryer will get them juicy and golden, before they're ready to bubble away in our rich, garlicky homemade sauce. Leave everything to mingle, turning halfway, until it's all ready to spoon over a fluffy portion of basmati rice.

Weekly Indulgence

Place all of the ingredients for the meatballs in a large bowl and mix together. Divide the mixture into 12 small meatballs. Each meatball should weigh approx. 45g.

Place the meatballs into the air fryer basket and air-fry at 200°C for 10 minutes until the meatballs are golden brown.

While the meatballs are cooking, place all of the sauce ingredients into a bowl and mix well. Transfer the sauce into the silicone liner or foil tray.

After 10 minutes, remove the meatballs from the air fryer and, using tongs, carefully place them into the liner or tray of sauce so they rest just on top of it. Place the tray into the air fryer and air-fry at 180°C for 20 minutes. Halfway through cooking, turn the meatballs and give the sauce a good stir.

After 20 minutes of the sauce bubbling away, the bake should be ready to serve along with rice or an accompaniment of your choice!

For freezing and reheating guidelines see page 17.

BAKES AND ROASTS

LASAGNE

🕐 **15 MINS**   🍲 **55 MINS + 10 MINS RESTING**   ✕ **SERVES 6**

FREEZE ME

BATCH COOK

DAIRY FREE

USE DF CHEESE

GLUTEN FREE

USE GF LASAGNE SHEETS, STOCK CUBES AND HENDERSON'S RELISH

PER SERVING:
248KCAL /11G CARBS

SPECIAL EQUIPMENT:
18cm (7in) square ovenproof dish or tin to fit your air fryer

low-calorie cooking spray
1 onion, peeled and diced
1 celery stick, chopped
1 carrot, peeled and chopped
2 garlic cloves, peeled and chopped
400g 5%-fat beef mince
1 tbsp dried mixed Italian herbs
1 tbsp Henderson's relish (or Worcestershire sauce)
1 courgette, diced
1 red pepper, deseeded and diced
1 green pepper, deseeded and diced
5 mushrooms, sliced
70g tomato puree
2 reduced-salt beef stock cubes
1 x 400g tin chopped tomatoes
200ml boiling water
6 lasagne sheets
60g reduced-fat mature Cheddar, finely grated
100g mozzarella, torn into large pieces
sea salt and freshly ground black pepper

TO ACCOMPANY
75g mixed salad (+15 kcal per serving)

TIP:

Don't overlap the lasagne sheets. If you do, they won't cook properly. Make sure all of the lasagne sheets are completely covered with the meat sauce so they don't burn.

Our classic Lasagne recipe is a firm favourite in our house, especially when we want a bit of comfort food in the middle of the week. It didn't take us long to figure out an easy way to cook it in an air fryer, and we've made it even cheesier than the original recipe! Instead of a white sauce, we've layered Cheddar and mozzarella on the top for a golden, melty topping you'll be dreaming about all day long. If your air fryer has a dual drawer you'll be able to make this straight in the drawer, otherwise you'll need an 18cm (7in) square or similar-sized ovenproof dish.

Everyday Light

Heat a pan over a medium heat and spray it with low-calorie cooking spray. Add the onion, celery, carrot and garlic and cook for a few minutes, until the vegetables start to soften. Add the mince and cook, stirring and breaking up the mince with a wooden spoon, until it starts to brown. Add the herbs and Henderson's relish or Worcestershire sauce and continue to cook for a few more minutes. Add the courgette and peppers and give the mixture a stir. Add the mushrooms and fry for about 5 minutes. Stir in the tomato puree, crumble in the stock cubes, add the tinned tomatoes and water, stir well.

Put the lid on the pan and simmer for 20 minutes, then remove the lid and simmer for another 10 minutes. Add seasoning to taste.

Spread a layer of the mince mixture on the bottom of the air fryer drawer or ovenproof dish, then add 2 lasagne sheets, without overlapping (see Tip). Repeat the layers until you've used all the lasagne sheets, finishing with meat sauce on top.

Air-fry at 170°C for 15 minutes, then carefully sprinkle the grated Cheddar over the top and finish with an even layer of the torn mozzarella. Cook for another 10 minutes. When cooked, the cheese should be nicely browned and a knife should easily slice through the lasagne sheets.

Remove the drawer or dish from the air fryer and allow to rest for around 10 minutes, so the lasagne is easier to portion. Cut into 6 portions and serve with a mixed salad.

For freezing and reheating guidelines see page 17.

BAKES AND ROASTS

FREEZE ME

BATCH COOK

DAIRY FREE

USE DF CHEESE

GLUTEN FREE

USE HENDERSON'S RELISH

HUNTER'S CHICKEN

🕐 **10 MINS**   🍲 **35 MINS**   ✕ **SERVES 4**

PER SERVING:
331 KCAL /11G CARBS

SPECIAL EQUIPMENT:
Air fryer liner
(stick) blender (optional)

4 skinless, boneless chicken
    breasts, approx. 150g each
4 bacon medallions
80g reduced-fat Cheddar,
    finely grated

FOR THE SAUCE
½ onion, peeled and diced
2 garlic cloves, peeled and
    crushed
1 x 400g tin chopped tomatoes
1 tbsp tomato puree
juice of ½ lemon
2 tbsp Worcestershire sauce (or
    Henderson's relish)
2 tbsp white wine vinegar
1 tbsp balsamic vinegar
1 tbsp Frank's Buffalo Wings Hot
    Sauce
1 tbsp BBQ seasoning
1 tsp mustard powder
¼ tsp smoked paprika
1 tsp granulated sweetener

TO ACCOMPANY
80g steamed green vegetables
    (+38 kcal per serving)

TIPS:

Use white granulated
sweetener that has the
same weight, texture and
sweetness as sugar.
You can use chilli powder or
normal paprika if you don't
have smoked paprika.

Everybody loves Hunter's Chicken! A pub-grub classic,
our twist on the family favourite cuts down on calories,
without spoiling any of the fun. The chicken is just as cheesy
as restaurant versions, topped with lower-calorie bacon
medallions and smothered in a rich, smoky, homemade BBQ
sauce. The beauty of using an air fryer is that your chicken
will cook while the sauce bubbles away, so it stays mouthwateringly juicy. You'll only need to check on it to flip it, add
the bacon and (importantly) sprinkle on the cheese!

Everyday Light

Remove the basket from the air fryer, or if you are unable to,
use a liner. Add all of the sauce ingredients into the air fryer
and mix.

Place the chicken breasts upside down on top of the sauce.
Air-fry at 180°C for 25 minutes, mixing the sauce and flipping
the chicken halfway through. Place the bacon medallions on
top of the chicken breasts. Cook for a further 5 minutes, until
the bacon is cooked.

When the time is up, check that the chicken is cooked and
white throughout by cutting into it with a sharp knife.

Optional: If you want a smooth sauce, remove the bacon-
covered chicken from the air fryer and blend the sauce,
either in a blender or using a stick blender in a suitable bowl.
Place the cooked bacon-covered chicken back in the air
fryer, then spoon or pour the sauce over the chicken breasts.

Sprinkle the cheese on top and air fry for a final 3–5 minutes,
until the cheese is melted and has a nice golden colour. Serve
hot with steamed green vegetables.

To freeze, cool fully and freeze in a freezerproof container.
For reheating guidelines see page 17.

BAKES AND ROASTS

FLUFFY JACKET POTATOES
with SPICY TUNA

🕐 **10 MINS**   🍲 **50–60 MINS**   ✕ **SERVES 4**

PER SERVING:
301 KCAL /51G CARBS

4 x 250g baking potatoes
low-calorie cooking spray
a good pinch of salt

FOR THE FILLING
2 x 145g tins tuna in spring
  water, drained
½ red pepper, deseeded and
  finely diced
½ red onion, peeled and finely
  diced
75g fat-free natural yoghurt
2 tbsp sriracha
juice of ½ lime
handful of fresh coriander,
  chopped
freshly ground black pepper
1 red chilli, thinly sliced
  (optional)

TO ACCOMPANY *(optional)*
75g mixed salad
  (+15 kcal per serving)

TIPS:

Jacket potato without filling is
214 kcal.

Pick a variety of potato well
suited to baking. King Edward
and Maris Piper are both
great choices, but you can
make it easy by buying the
packs of baking potatoes from
supermarkets. You know these
will be good bakers, and they
are all a uniform size and around
the correct weight for this recipe.

Cooking jacket potatoes in the air fryer gives you crispy skin and gorgeously fluffy centres every time. If that isn't impressive enough, it'll save 20–30 minutes, compared to baking them in the oven. That's a win-win if you ask us! You can follow these instructions to make the perfect potatoes, then use them as a side dish, or top them with your favourite filling. We've included a quick recipe for a spicy tuna filling, with crunchy red pepper and onion and a fiery sauce made with sriracha to liven up lunchtime!

Everyday Light ───────────

Wash and thoroughly dry the potatoes. Pierce each potato a few times with a fork, then spray with low-calorie cooking spray, sprinkle over the salt, and rub it into the skin.

Place the potatoes into the air fryer basket and air-fry at 200°C for 50 minutes, turning the potatoes halfway through. To test the potatoes are cooked, insert a skewer or knife into the centre of the potato. Once through the crisp skin, it should slide in easily. If it is still a little hard, air-fry for another 10 minutes, or until cooked.

While the potato cooks, mix all of the filling ingredients, except the sliced chilli, if using, in a bowl. You can add more sriracha if you like things very spicy.

When the potatoes are cooked, slice down the middle and fill with the spicy tuna.

Top with the sliced chilli, if using, and serve with a mixed salad, if you like.

LIGHT BITES

VEGGIE

VEGAN

DAIRY FREE

GLUTEN FREE

AIR FRYER CHICKPEAS

🕐 **5 MINS**   🧺 **14 MINS**   ✕ **SERVES 2**

PER SERVING:
259 KCAL /36G CARBS

1 x 400g tin chickpeas
low-calorie cooking spray
seasoning mix of choice (see below)

SMOKY PAPRIKA (253 KCAL)
1 tsp smoked paprika,
    sweet or hot
1 tsp garlic granules
½ tsp salt

GARLIC AND HERB (252 KCAL)
1 tsp garlic granules
½ tsp dried basil
½ tsp dried oregano
½ tsp salt

MOROCCAN SPICED (255 KCAL)
1 tsp ground sumac
1 tsp garlic granules
½ tsp salt

SWEET CINNAMON (259 KCAL)
½ tsp ground cinnamon
½ tsp salt
1 ½ tsp granulated sweetener

In a hurry for a light nibble? These air-fried chickpeas make for a scrummy alternative to nuts, and they're ready to snack on in under 20 minutes. Don't worry if you fancy a change of flavour from time to time – there are 4 different homemade spice blends to choose from! We've kept things super simple by sticking to staple herbs and spices you're likely to have in your store cupboard already. Try flavouring with Smoky Paprika, Garlic and Herb or Moroccan Spiced from the savoury selection, or mix things up with a Sweet Cinnamon batch.

Weekly Indulgence

Drain and rinse the tinned chickpeas. Shake dry, then lay on a plate with clean kitchen paper and pat dry. Spray the dry chickpeas with low-calorie cooking spray. If making one of the savoury flavours, add all the herbs and spices. For sweet cinnamon flavour, add only the cinnamon.

Add the coated chickpeas to the air fryer basket and spread out across the bottom. Air-fry at 200°C for 14 minutes, shaking halfway, until the chickpeas are golden and crispy. Keep an eye on the chickpeas for the last few minutes to make sure they don't burn.

For the savoury flavours, tip into a bowl and serve. For the sweet cinnamon flavour, tip into a bowl and add the salt and sweetener, shaking to coat evenly before serving.

TIP:

Use white granulated sweetener that has the same weight, texture and sweetness as sugar.

VEGGIE

BATCH COOK

GLUTEN FREE
USE GF BREADCRUMBS

VIKING CROQUETTES

🕐 **20 MINS**　🍲 **10 MINS**　✕ **SERVES 8**

PER CROQUETTE:
128 KCAL /16G CARBS

SPECIAL EQUIPMENT:
Potato masher

750g potatoes, peeled
  and diced
low-calorie cooking spray
1 medium onion, peeled and
  finely diced
80g reduced-fat mature
  Cheddar, grated
2 tsp Henderson's relish
2 tsp skimmed milk
1 tsp mustard powder
1 whole egg plus two egg yolks
70g breadcrumbs
sea salt and freshly ground
  black pepper

TO ACCOMPANY *(optional)*
1 tbsp tomato ketchup
  (+15 kcal per tbsp)

Golden on the outside and delightfully fluffy in the middle, these Viking Croquettes are the dish everybody's talking about. Inspired by the bold flavours from our viral Viking Toast recipe, we've combined punchy mustard with cheese, onion and creamy mashed potatoes, before rolling it in a crunchy layer of breadcrumbs. The results are gloriously crispy, with a heavenly centre that goes down a treat with a whole host of different mains.

Everyday Light

Cook the potatoes in a pan of boiling water over a medium heat for around 15 minutes, or until a knife slides easily through a piece of potato. Drain well and return to the pan. Mash well with a potato masher and set to one side to cool.

Spray a frying pan with low-calorie cooking spray. Add the onion and cook over a medium heat until it starts to soften.

Add the cooked onion to the mashed potato, along with the cheese, Henderson's relish, milk, mustard powder, 1 egg yolk and a pinch each of salt and pepper. Mix together thoroughly.

On a plate, spread out the breadcrumbs.

In a separate bowl, beat the egg with the remaining egg yolk.

Separate the mash mixture into 16 evenly sized portions and roll each into a sausage shape.

Dip a croquette into the egg, then place it on top of the breadcrumbs and gently roll from side to side, making sure the croquette is completely covered. Repeat for the rest of the croquettes.

Place the croquettes in the air fryer basket, ensuring that they do not touch each other. You may need to cook these in batches, depending on the size of your air fryer. Air-fry at 180°C for 10 minutes, carefully turning half way, until they are golden and crispy.

Allow to cool for a few minutes before serving.

TIPS:

If the croquettes lose their shape when dipped into the egg mixture, you can reshape them once they are covered in breadcrumbs before cooking in the air fryer.

Using slightly damp hands when shaping the croquettes will stop them sticking to your fingers.

SWEET POTATO *and* FETA PARCELS

🕐 **10 MINS** 🍲 **11 MINS** ✕ **MAKES 12**

VEGGIE
USE VEGETARIAN FETA

VEGAN
USE VEGAN FETA

DAIRY FREE
USE DF FETA

PER PARCEL:
113 KCAL /17G CARBS

SPECIAL EQUIPMENT:
Potato masher

250g sweet potato, peeled and diced
200g reduced-fat feta cheese
1 tbsp grated lemon zest
¼ tsp salt
½ tsp onion granules
¼ tsp garlic granules
½ tsp dried oregano
6 single sheets of filo pastry
low-calorie cooking spray

Sweet potato and feta is a delicious combination to begin with, and we've brought the flavours to life even more with zingy lemon zest. Once your filling is tightly wrapped into 12 little filo pastry bundles, nestle them in your air fryer to crisp up. Five minutes later, you're left with a crunchy, cheesy snack that'll have you coming back for more!

Everyday Light

Cook the diced sweet potato in a pan of boiling water over a medium heat for around 6 minutes, or until a knife slides easily through a piece. Drain the sweet potato well and place in a large bowl. Mash and set to one side to cool.

Into a separate bowl, crumble the feta. Add the lemon zest to the feta. Mix in the salt, onion granules, garlic granules and dried oregano. Combine the sweet potato with the feta mixture and fold together.

Take a sheet of filo pastry and lay it down with the longest side closest to you. Spray evenly with low-calorie cooking spray, especially the edges. Place another sheet of pastry on top and spray again with low-calorie cooking spray. Cut in half top to bottom and then cut each half again top to bottom so you have 4 long rectangles, each approx. 23 x 6cm (9 x 2¼in).

Take one of the rectangles and place a tablespoon of the filling in the centre of one end. Fold one corner of the pastry diagonally over to enclose the filling. Press down the edges to seal. Fold diagonally again, and press down the edges. Repeat until you reach the end of the pastry rectangle and you have a triangular pastry parcel. Continue with the other 3 rectangles. Repeat until you have used all 6 sheets of filo pastry and you have 12 pastry parcels.

Place the parcels in the air fryer, ensuring they do not touch each other, and spray with low-calorie cooking spray. You may need to cook these in batches, depending on the size of your air fryer. Air-fry at 180°C for 5 minutes.

Carefully remove from the air fryer and leave to cool for a few minutes before serving.

TIP:

Leave the feta out of the packet on some kitchen paper when you start to prepare the sweet potato, to allow any excess moisture to drain.

SMOKY BACON SCOTCH EGGS

🕐 **25 MINS**   🍲 **20 MINS**   ✕ **SERVES 4**

PER SERVING:
257 KCAL /11G CARBS

SPECIAL EQUIPMENT:
Food processor or mini chopper

4 medium eggs, at room temperature
6 smoked bacon medallions, roughly chopped
4 reduced-fat sausages
1 tsp smoked sweet paprika
½ tsp garlic granules
40g wholemeal bread, blitzed into crumbs
freshly ground black pepper
1 tsp cornflour
low-calorie cooking spray

TO ACCOMPANY *(optional)*
1 tbsp mustard (+10 kcal per tbsp)

We've taken inspiration from one of your picnic favourites to create the ultimate grab-and-go snack: Smoky Bacon Scotch Eggs! We boil our eggs for 6 minutes for a slightly soft yolk, but there's nothing to stop you serving up a hard-boiled centre, if you prefer. As long as they're wrapped in our moreish combination of bacon, sausage, smoked paprika, garlic and breadcrumbs, you can't go wrong!

Weekly Indulgence ——————————

Bring a pan of water to the boil over a high heat and use a spoon to carefully lower the eggs into the water. Reduce the heat to a simmer and cook to your liking – 5 minutes for soft yolk, 8 minutes for hard-boiled. When cooked, remove from the pan using a slotted spoon and plunge into a bowl of cold water to stop the eggs cooking.

While the eggs cool, make your coating. Place the bacon in a food processor or mini chopper and blitz in pulses, until finely chopped with a texture like sausage meat. Squeeze the meat out of the sausages, discarding the skins, and place in a bowl with the bacon. Add the smoked sweet paprika, garlic granules and 4 tablespoons of the breadcrumbs. Season with black pepper and mix well until thoroughly combined.

Carefully peel the cooled eggs and pat dry with kitchen paper. Place the remaining breadcrumbs in a bowl.

Divide the sausage and bacon mixture into 4 equal-sized balls. Take one egg and lightly dust it with cornflour. Take one ball of sausage and bacon mixture and flatten slightly in your hands. Place the dusted egg in the middle and carefully wrap the sausage and bacon mixture around to completely encase the egg. Be gentle!

Place the egg in the remaining breadcrumbs and roll until well coated. Lightly press the breadcrumbs to ensure they stick. Place to one side and repeat with the remaining eggs.

Spray the air fryer basket with low-calorie cooking spray. Place the eggs into the basket and spray each egg well with low-calorie cooking spray. Air-fry at 200°C for 12 minutes, or until crisp and golden. Serve warm or cold.

CHEESE, ONION *and* SWEETCORN-STUFFED PEPPERS

🕐 **5 MINS**   🍲 **15 MINS**   ✕ **SERVES 4**

PER SERVING:
155 KCAL /14G CARBS

4 medium mixed peppers
165g reduced-fat cream cheese
120g drained tinned sweetcorn
½ tsp Dijon mustard
2 spring onions, trimmed and
  finely chopped
20g reduced-fat Cheddar,
  grated
freshly ground black pepper

TO SERVE *(optional)*
small handful fresh basil leaves

There's nothing humble about these bright and colourful stuffed peppers! To make them into a vibrant, satisfying, slimming-friendly light bite, we've filled them to the brim with crunchy sweetcorn, reduced-fat cream cheese and punchy Dijon mustard . . . and the flavours don't stop there! All topped off with spring onions and an irresistible layer of melty reduced-fat Cheddar cheese, they're bold and delicious for only 155 calories each.

Everyday Light

Lay each pepper on its side and slice in half horizontally. Remove the seeds from the inside of the peppers.

In a bowl, mix together the cream cheese, sweetcorn, Dijon mustard, spring onion and black pepper to taste.

Place equal amounts of the mixture into the pepper halves.

Place the 8 pepper halves into the air fryer and air-fry at 180°C for 10 minutes.

After 10 minutes, sprinkle each pepper evenly with the Cheddar. Cook for a further 5 minutes.

Carefully remove the cooked peppers from the air fryer. Garnish with fresh basil leaves, if you like, and serve!

USE GF WRAPS AND HENDERSON'S RELISH

SAUSAGE ROLLS

🕐 **10 MINS** 🍲 **20 MINS** ✕ **SERVES 6**

PER SERVING:
170 KCAL /12G CARBS

400g 5%-fat pork mince
½ onion, peeled and finely chopped
2 eggs, beaten
1 dash Worcestershire sauce (or Henderson's relish)
1½ tsp freshly chopped thyme, or ½ tsp dried
1½ tsp freshly chopped sage, or ½ tsp dried
1½ tsp freshly chopped parsley, or ½ tsp dried
½ tsp mustard powder
1 tsp sea salt
½ tsp freshly ground black pepper
3 low-calorie tortilla wraps

Our favourite thing about making sausage rolls at home is knowing exactly what's in them, so there's no worrying about hidden nasties! The savoury filling is just as moreish as bakery-bought versions, thanks to a blend of store-cupboard herbs and spices, reduced-fat pork mince and a splash of Worcestershire sauce. Instead of full-fat pastry, you'll bundle your ingredients into low-calorie tortilla-wrap rolls, and bake them to golden perfection in the air fryer. The only question is, will you serve them with red or brown sauce?

Everyday Light

Place the mince, onion, half of the beaten egg, Worcestershire sauce, herbs and seasonings into a bowl and mix thoroughly.

Divide the mixture into 6 equal sausage shapes. Place the sausages in the air fryer and air-fry at 200°C for 10 minutes.

Remove the sausages from the air fryer and leave them until cool enough to handle.

Lay a low-calorie tortilla wrap flat on a work surface and brush all over the top with some of the remaining beaten egg. Place 2 sausages at one end and roll them up tightly in the wrap. Cut the wraps in half. Give them a gentle squish to flatten slightly to prevent them rolling around in the air fryer. You can cut the ends off the wrap just to tidy them up a little and make slits across the top if you like. Repeat with the other 2 wraps.

Place the 6 sausage rolls into the air fryer and brush each one with the remaining beaten egg. Cook for 10 minutes, or until they are golden brown.

Allow to cool for a few minutes before serving. You can also freeze these as soon as they are cold, just place them in a container or bag that is suitable for freezing. For standard defrosting and reheating guidelines see page 17.

USE GF BREAD
AND HENDERSON'S
RELISH

POTATO DOGS

🕐 **20 MINS**   🍲 **35 MINS**   ✕ **SERVES 6**

PER SERVING:
329 KCAL /41G CARBS

SPECIAL EQUIPMENT:
Potato masher
Food processor

FOR THE SAUSAGES
500g 5%-fat pork mince
1 tsp garlic granules or garlic
   powder
1 tbsp Henderson's relish (or
   Worcestershire sauce)
¼ tsp mustard powder
low-calorie cooking spray
sea salt and freshly ground
   black pepper

FOR THE POTATO
1kg potatoes, peeled and
   quartered
1 large onion, peeled and finely
   diced
1 tsp garlic granules or garlic
   powder
120g wholemeal bread, blitzed
   into crumbs
1 medium egg, beaten

A cross between mashed potatoes, hot dogs and sausage rolls, our Potato Dogs are delicious hot or cold. The centre is a homemade sausage, made with reduced-fat pork mince to help keep the calories down. Wrapped up in creamy mashed potatoes and cooked until golden, these are a treat for lunch (and they're perfect for picnics too!).

Special Occasion

Put the pork mince, garlic granules or powder, Henderson's relish or Worcestershire sauce, mustard powder and a generous pinch each of salt and pepper into a bowl and mix thoroughly with your hands.

Shape into 6 long, thin sausage shapes and place on a piece of foil that's been sprayed with low-calorie cooking spray. Place into the air fryer basket and air-fry at 180°C for 10 minutes. Once done, remove them from the air fryer and leave to one side until they are cool enough to handle.

While the sausages are cooking, place the potatoes into a large saucepan and cover with cold water. Place over a medium heat and bring to the boil, then reduce the heat to a simmer and cook for 15–20 minutes, or until the potatoes are tender. Drain the potatoes and set aside.

While the potatoes and sausages are cooling, place a frying pan over a medium heat and spray with low-calorie cooking spray. Add the onion and cook for 5 minutes until softened.

Mash the potatoes and add the cooked onion, garlic granules or powder and season with salt and pepper to taste.

When the potato has cooled enough to handle, mix in the breadcrumbs and half of the beaten egg. Take one of the cooled sausages and use your hands to shape the potato mixture around it. Repeat until all the sausages are covered.

Place the potato dogs back onto the piece of foil and place into the air fryer. Brush the tops with the remaining beaten egg and spray with low-calorie cooking spray. Air-fry for 15 minutes or until golden brown. Serve with a dip of your choice!

For freezing and reheating guidelines see page 17.

PIZZA SWIRLS

🕙 **10 MINS**   🍲 **8 MINS**   ✕ **MAKES 16**

PER SWIRL:
50 KCAL /4.9G CARBS

1 tbsp passata
1½ tsp tomato puree
pinch of garlic granules
160g ready-rolled light puff pastry sheet
20g reduced-fat mature Cheddar, finely grated
15g Parmesan cheese, finely grated
25g lean cooked sliced ham, finely diced
5g fresh basil leaves, stalks removed and roughly torn
sea salt and freshly ground black pepper

TIPS:

Make sure that the basil leaves are completely dry before using, otherwise they may make the pastry soggy.

Most cooked ham is gluten-free, but do check as some isn't. If you prefer, you could use other cooked meats, such as bacon or chicken, instead of ham.

FAN FAVOURITE

'Easy to put together, especially when you have the ingredients to hand in your fridge and cupboard. An easy go-to lunch served with salad. Very tasty. You can't go wrong with a Pinch of Nom recipe.'
Charlotte Johnson

When you've got a hankering for pizza, these delicious puff pastry bites are just the ticket. With a tomatoey, cheesy ham and basil filling, they're best served warm as part of a buffet spread (or you can stash them away in your lunchbox for a light snack!). To cut down on fuss and calories, you can't beat ready-rolled sheets of light puff pastry. Wrap up your pizza-inspired filling, slice, and let your air fryer do the rest of the work. Remember, you can always mix things up with different fillings to suit your go-to pizza order!

Everyday Light ─────────────────────

Place the passata, tomato puree and garlic granules in a small bowl and mix well.

Unroll the pastry sheet, leaving it on the greaseproof paper. Spread the tomato mixture over the pastry sheet in a thin layer, leaving a 1cm (½in) gap along one long edge.

Sprinkle the Cheddar and Parmesan over in an even layer, leaving a 1cm (½in) gap along the long edge. Spread the ham over the cheese in an even layer, leaving a 1cm (½in) gap along the long edge. Sprinkle the basil leaves over the ham, again leaving the gap along the long edge. Season well with salt and pepper.

Roll up the pastry tightly, starting with the long edge without the 1cm (½in) gap and using the greaseproof paper to help you. Keep rolling it up until you have a 'Swiss roll'. When you have finished rolling the pastry, make sure it is seam-side down, then use a large serrated knife (such as a bread knife) to cut it into 16 spiral-shaped slices.

Carefully transfer the slices to the air fryer basket, leaving gaps between each, and press the seam on each to ensure a good seal. You may need to do this in batches, depending on the size of your air fryer. Air-fry at 190°C for 8 minutes until golden and crisp.

These swirls are best served warm. You can freeze them after baking, just allow them to cool fully and place in a freezerproof container. For standard defrosting and reheating guidelines see page 17.

LIGHT BITES

VEGGIE

VEGAN

USE VEGAN CHEESE
AND VEGAN
MAYONNAISE

DAIRY
FREE

USE DF CHEESE

GLUTEN
FREE

USE GF BREAD

GOUDA *and* CRANBERRY TOASTIE

🕐 **5 MINS**　🍲 **8 MINS**　✕ **SERVES 1**

PER SERVING:
448 KCAL /32G CARBS

4 tsp reduced-fat mayonnaise
2 medium slices wholemeal
　bread
20g Gouda cheese, sliced
1 tsp cranberry sauce

How 'Gouda' does this air-fried toastie look? We couldn't put together a whole book of air fryer recipes and not have a go at making the ultimate cheesy lunchtime treat. Instead of the traditional pairing of cheese and chutney, we've spooned sweet cranberry sauce inside this one. Paired with the nutty, caramel flavour of the Gouda, every bite is a delight. You'll notice there's no butter in the ingredients list – we've spread reduced-fat mayonnaise on the bread for this recipe instead, as it makes it crisp up a treat in the air fryer!

Special Occasion

Spread a teaspoon of mayonnaise on both sides of the bread slices.

Place the Gouda on one slice of bread, then take the other slice of bread and spread the cranberry sauce over one side. Place that slice of bread on top of the Gouda, cranberry side down, to make a sandwich.

Place a piece of non-stick baking paper on top of the sandwich and roll gently with a rolling pin in order to flatten the bread slightly. This will stop the toastie coming apart in the air fryer.

Remove the baking paper and place the sandwich into the air fryer. Air-fry at 200°C for 8 minutes, turning the toastie halfway through. Serve!

VEGGIE

USE VEGETARIAN
PARMESAN/
ITALIAN-STYLE
HARD CHEESE

FREEZE ME

BATCH COOK

DAIRY FREE

USE DF CHEESE

GLUTEN FREE

USE GF
STOCK CUBE

CHEESY ROASTED VEGETABLE SOUP

🕐 **15 MINS**   🍲 **30 MINS**   ✕ **SERVES 4**

PER SERVING:
132 KCAL / 18G CARBS

SPECIAL EQUIPMENT:
Blender or food processor

1 large carrot, approx.
  140g, sliced
2 peppers, any colour,
  deseeded and roughly
  chopped
1 red onion, peeled and
  cut into wedges
1 courgette, roughly chopped
200g butternut squash,
  peeled and diced
2 tomatoes, cut in half
3 garlic cloves, peeled
  and cut in half
2 tbsp harissa paste, such as
  Al'fez Harissa Paste (30g)
low-calorie cooking spray
600ml vegetable stock
  (1 vegetable stock cube
  dissolved in 600ml
  boiling water)
180g reduced-fat cream cheese
1 tsp grated Italian-style
  hard cheese
sea salt and freshly ground
  black pepper

TO ACCOMPANY *(optional)*
Cheese and Chive Scones
  (+94 kcal per scone)

Soup . . . in an air fryer? Okay, so you'll finish off this recipe in a blender, but air-fried roasted vegetables are the key to the gorgeous garlicky flavour. Creamy, cheesy and comforting, this is a hearty bowl of goodness that'll warm you right up on a chilly day. A couple of tablespoons of harissa paste give our soup a little kick, and you can add more or less to suit how spicy you like it. Serve with a warm Cheese and Chive Scone (page 164) and you're in for a treat!

Everyday Light ─────────────────────

Place all the chopped veg in a large bowl, along with the garlic. Coat with the harissa paste, spray with low-calorie cooking spray and season with some salt and pepper. Mix well and place in the air fryer basket. Air-fry at 200°C for 20–30 minutes, or until the veg is cooked and nicely browned.

When cooked, add the veg, hot stock and cream cheese to the blender or food processor and blitz until smooth. Taste and season if required.

If the soup is too thick for you, add some boiling water. If the soup isn't hot enough, gently heat it in a pan on the stove.

To serve, sprinkle a quarter teaspoon of grated Italian-style hard cheese on each portion and serve with Cheese and Chive Scones, if you like.

For freezing and reheating guidelines see page 17.

LIGHT BITES

VEGGIE

FREEZE ME

BATCH COOK

GLUTEN FREE

USE GF SANDWICH THINS

CHEESE *and* ONION BAKES

🕐 **10 MINS**   🍲 **7 MINS**   ✕ **MAKES 4**

PER BAKE:
220 KCAL /20G CARBS

120g reduced-fat mature Cheddar, finely grated
½ medium onion, peeled and finely chopped
4 soft sliced white or brown sandwich thins
1 medium egg, beaten
sea salt and freshly ground black pepper

TO ACCOMPANY *(optional)*
Air Fryer Chips (+169 kcal per serving). Follow our recipe for Loaded Cheeseburger Fries on page 76.

TIP:

Leave the bakes to cool on a wire rack rather than in the air fryer, otherwise the bases may become soggy.

FAN FAVOURITE

'The results are melt-in-the-middle deliciousness, for a fraction of the calories you'd find at the bakery. You will love these and so will the family . . . a bake to make time after time.'
Adele Sutcliffe

For these simple homemade bakes, we've said goodbye to pastry and lowered the calories with sandwich thins. Far better for you and your budget than bakery-bought versions, you'll only need a super-short list of ingredients to rustle up these bakes. For our gooey centre, we've filled our 'pastry' with a heavenly combo of reduced-fat Cheddar and onion, and baked it in the air fryer until golden. Tuck into them as a grab-and-go snack, or plate them up with a side of chips for a hearty midweek dinner!

Weekly Indulgence

Place the cheese and onion in a medium mixing bowl and season with salt and pepper. Stir until evenly mixed.

Split the sandwich thins in half and lay them out on a chopping board. Divide the cheese and onion mixture into 4 equal portions. Place a portion of the mixture onto 4 sandwich thin halves. Pile the mixture up in the middle, then gently press down to form a square, leaving a 1cm (½in) gap around the edge.

Brush beaten egg around the edge and place one of the remaining sandwich thin halves on top of the filling. Press the centre of the lid down gently with a flat hand, then press around the edges to seal. Use a fork to crimp the edges and seal well. Repeat until you've made 4 bakes.

Brush all over the tops of the bakes with the remaining egg (you may not need all of it). Place the bakes into the air fryer basket, making sure the egg-coated side is facing upward. You may need to do this in batches, depending on the size of your air fryer.

Air-fry at 180°C for 7 minutes. When cooked they will be golden brown on the outside and gooey inside. Carefully remove from the air fryer and place on a wire rack. You can serve these hot or cold, alone, or with a crisp mixed salad or other accompaniment of your choice.

For freezing and reheating guidelines see page 17.

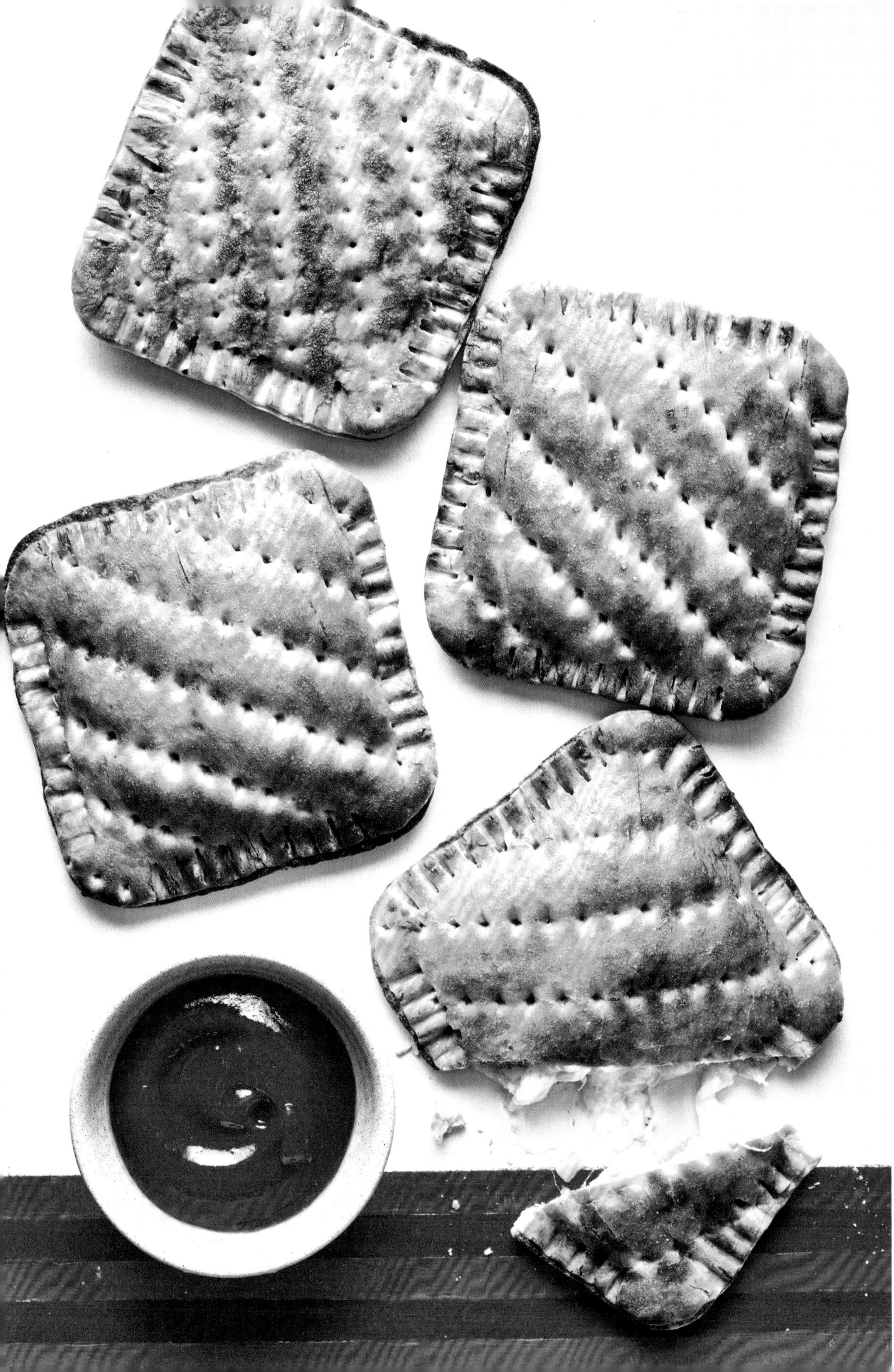

CHEESE *and* CHIVE SCONES

⏱ **15 MINS** 🍲 **8 MINS** ✕ **MAKES 14**

PER SCONE:
94 KCAL /13G CARBS

SPECIAL EQUIPMENT:
6cm (2 ½in)-diameter plain pastry cutter

250g self-raising flour, plus extra for dusting
1 tsp baking powder
25g reduced-fat spread
large bunch of chives, finely chopped
100g reduced-fat mature Cheddar, grated
1 medium egg
120ml skimmed milk
low-calorie cooking spray
sea salt and freshly ground black pepper

Can you believe these fluffy cheese scones are less than 100 calories each? For the cheesiest possible flavour, use a really mature Cheddar, and serve them warm, straight from the air fryer basket. Ready in 8 minutes, our crispy, golden-brown scones are delicious on their own, but even better served with a steaming hot bowl of Cheesy Roasted Vegetable Soup (page 160).

Everyday Light

Sift the flour and baking powder into a large bowl. Add the reduced-fat spread and, using your fingertips, rub into the flour until the mixture resembles fine breadcrumbs.

Stir in the chives and three-quarters of the grated cheese and season well with salt and pepper. Beat the egg and milk together in a small jug.

Make a well in the centre of the bowl and add the milk and egg mixture. Stir with a spoon or round-bladed knife until the mix comes together. Lightly flour your work surface and tip out the scone mix. Lightly knead for a couple of seconds to form a soft dough. Do not over knead, as this will cause the scones to be tough.

Roll out the dough, using a floured rolling pin, to around 1cm (½in) thick. Using the pastry cutter, cut out scones, reforming the scraps and rolling out again, until all the dough has been used. You should get 14 scones out of the mixture. Sprinkle the remaining cheese on top of the scones.

Spray the air fryer basket with low-calorie cooking spray and place the scones directly into the basket, leaving a little gap between each scone. You may need to do this in batches, depending on the size of your air fryer. Air-fry at 200°C for 8 minutes, until crisp and golden outside.

The scones can be frozen in sealed bags when cool. To defrost, remove from the bag, cover and leave for 1–2 hours to defrost. These can be eaten cold but are even better when popped in the air fryer for 2–3 minutes to reheat.

TIPS:

These are delicious served warm, straight from the air fryer, but are also great served at room temperature.

Can be stored for up to 5 days in an airtight tin.

LIGHT BITES

VEGGIE

USE VEGETARIAN
PARMESAN/
ITALIAN-STYLE
HARD CHEESE

**GLUTEN
FREE**

USE GF
BREADCRUMBS

BROCAULI BITES

🕐 **10 MINS**   🍲 **8–12 MINS**   ✕ **SERVES 4**

PER SERVING:
107 KCAL /13G CARBS

2 tsp garlic powder
2 tsp grated Parmesan or
    Italian-style hard cheese
pinch of salt
40g panko breadcrumbs
1 medium egg
160g cauliflower, cut into small
    bite-size florets
160g broccoli, cut into small
    bite-size florets
low-calorie cooking spray

FOR THE DIP
1 tbsp reduced-fat mayonnaise
1 tbsp sriracha

TO ACCOMPANY *(optional)*
Char-Siu-Style Pork Tenderloin
    (+288 kcal per serving)

A colourful combination of broccoli and cauliflower, these Brocauli Bites will take your midweek menu up a notch. To keep them crispy for fewer calories, toss panko breadcrumbs with garlic powder and grated Parmesan, then coat your veggies in the indulgent-tasting, cheesy crumb. So crunchy and satisfying, these jazzed-up florets are also perfect to snack on when you're in the mood for a light, savoury bite. We've even included how to whip up the perfect sriracha-infused mayo for dipping!

Everyday Light ———————————

First make the dip. Mix the mayonnaise and sriracha together in a small bowl and set aside. In a separate bowl, add the garlic powder, Parmesan, salt and panko breadcrumbs. Stir well and set aside with the sriracha mayo.

Crack the egg into a large bowl and beat with a fork until it is well mixed.

Toss the cauliflower and broccoli florets in the egg, making sure they are all well coated. Place them on a tray or large plate and spray them with some low-calorie cooking spray.

Sprinkle the breadcrumb mix over the florets. Coat them as well as you can by pressing the breadcrumbs onto the florets to make them stick.

Place the cauliflower and broccoli into the air fryer basket and sprinkle over any breadcrumbs that didn't stick. Air-fry at 180°C for 8–12 minutes until the veg is just cooked and the panko coating is crisp and golden.

Carefully remove from the air fryer basket and serve with the sriracha mayo. These are delicious served as a side for Char-Siu-Style Pork Tenderloin.

VEGGIE

GLUTEN FREE

USE GF PLAIN FLOUR

BLOOMING ONION
with DIPPING SAUCE

🕐 **10 MINS**   🍲 **15 MINS**   ✕ **SERVES 2**

PER SERVING:
245 KCAL /28G CARBS

2 medium onions
70ml semi-skimmed milk
1 medium egg
30g plain flour
1 tsp garlic granules
1 tsp onion granules
1 tsp chilli powder
1 tsp paprika
low-calorie cooking spray
sea salt and freshly ground
   black pepper

FOR THE DIPPING SAUCE
2 tbsp reduced-fat mayonnaise
1 tsp sriracha

When you've got guests to impress, this is exactly the type of recipe you need on your menu! Low on effort and big on wow factor, the ingredients are simple, and the end result is delicious. If you've ever had a blooming onion in a restaurant, you'll know they're typically deep-fried, but your air fryer will work wonders on our lightly-battered, mildly-spiced version. Whip up a quick sriracha mayonnaise, ready to dunk in the crispy golden onion petals.

Weekly Indulgence ———————

First, prepare the onions. Take one onion and slice off the end that does not contain the root. Peel the onion. Place the onion flat side down, so the root side is facing upwards. Using a sharp knife, make a slice downwards starting 1cm (½in) from the root. Keep making slices, finger-width apart, until you have sliced all the way around. Repeat with the second onion. Open up each onion so it looks like a flower.

Place the milk and egg in a large measuring jug and beat with a fork or whisk until well combined.

Add the flour, garlic granules, onion granules, chilli powder, paprika and a pinch each of salt and pepper to a large mixing bowl. Mix together thoroughly with a fork.

Place one of the prepared onions into the flour mixture. Spoon the flour mixture over the onion so it is covered thoroughly. Place the onion into the egg mixture and then back into the flour mixture. Cover the onion again with the flour mixture. Repeat with the second onion.

Place the onions in the air fryer basket and spray with low-calorie cooking spray. Air-fry at 180°C for 15 minutes, but check after 12 minutes.

While the onions are cooking, mix together the mayonnaise and sriracha in a bowl to make the dipping sauce.

Once they are golden and cooked through, remove the onions from the air fryer and serve with the dipping sauce.

TIP:

Take your time with the onion slicing, and ensure your knife is really sharp for best results.

LIGHT BITES

ALOO BORA

🕐 **20 MINS**   🍲 **30 MINS**   ✗ **MAKES 16**

PER POTATO CAKE:
44 KCAL /7.6G CARBS

SPECIAL EQUIPMENT:
Potato masher or potato ricer,
food processor

500g potatoes, peeled
  and quartered
low-calorie cooking spray
1 small onion, peeled and
  finely diced
1 chilli, deseeded and
  finely diced
1 medium egg
1 tsp ground turmeric
1 tsp ground coriander
15g fresh coriander, finely
  chopped
60g wholemeal bread,
  blitzed into crumbs
sea salt and freshly ground
  black pepper

TO ACCOMPANY *(optional)*
1 tbsp mango chutney
  (+48 kcal per tbsp)

These eye-catching little Aloo Bora potato cakes are absolutely spot on for a curry-night spread. To make our light, bright mixture, we've used a potato masher to combine colourful turmeric with fiery chilli and fragrant coriander. Once they're in the air fryer, you won't have long to wait before they're delightfully crisp and golden. Tuck into them as a side dish, or you can even take them on the go – they're yummy served hot or cold!

Everyday Light ──────────────

Place the potatoes in a pan of boiling salted water, bring back to the boil and simmer for 15 minutes until they are cooked. Drain the potatoes well, then mash until smooth. You can use a potato masher or potato ricer to do this. Set aside.

Spray a small frying pan with some low-calorie cooking spray, place over a medium heat and gently fry the onion for 5 minutes until it begins to soften. Set aside to cool for a minute.

Add the cooked mash, onion and the rest of the ingredients into a bowl, season with salt and pepper and mix well. Take a golf-ball-sized amount of the mixture and gently shape into a small patty. Place onto a plate. Repeat until all the mixture is used, you should have around 16 patties.

Spray the tops of the patties with low-calorie cooking spray and place topside down in the air fryer basket. Spray again with low-calorie cooking spray so both sides have now been coated. Air-fry at 180°C for 10 minutes. You may need to do this in batches, depending on the size of your air fryer. When done, they should have a nice brown colour on the outside.

Serve warm or cold with some mango chutney for dipping, if you like.

For freezing and reheating guidelines see page 17.

LIGHT BITES

TIP:

These are brilliant
for picnics.

SWEET TREATS

CHERRY BAKEWELL SLICES

🕐 **10 MINS**   🍳 **18 MINS**   ✕ **SERVES 12**

PER SLICE:
91 KCAL /13G CARBS

SPECIAL EQUIPMENT:
Electric whisk, 15cm (6in)
square baking tin

100g self-raising flour
40g reduced-fat spread
1 medium egg, beaten
1 tsp almond extract
2 tbsp low-calorie syrup
2 tbsp ground almonds
3 tbsp granulated sweetener
1 tsp baking powder
40g glacé cherries, roughly
  chopped
5g flaked almonds

These beautiful Cherry Bakewell Slices will make your afternoon tea break feel extra special, for only 91 calories per fruity slice. We've kept our recipe far lighter than you'd expect, thanks to a handful of nifty slimming-friendly ingredients. Our top tip for the perfect texture? Undercook them ever so slightly and leave to cool in the tin before slicing – it'll carry on the cooking process, so you get an irresistible, squidgy-in-the-middle batch every time.

Everyday Light ─────────────────

First, line the bottom of the baking tin with baking parchment or greaseproof paper.

Place all of the ingredients, apart from the cherries and flaked almonds, into a large mixing bowl and mix thoroughly using an electric whisk. Keep whisking until the mixture is no longer grainy.

Stir in the chopped cherries and pour the mixture into the lined baking tin. Scatter over the flaked almonds. Place in the air fryer and air-fry at 160°C for 14–18 minutes, until golden but still slightly squidgy. Leave in the tin to cool.

Once cool, remove from the tin and cut into 12 even-sized pieces.

You can freeze the slices once cold, in a plastic freezerproof container, separated by sheets of non-stick baking paper. Defrost at room temperature.

TIPS:

Use white granulated sweetener that has the same weight, texture and sweetness as sugar.

We've used ground almonds and glacé cherries to give that instantly recognizable Bakewell flavour, but you could use fresh cherries.

SWEET TREATS

BISCOFF BANANA BITES

🕐 **10 MINS** 🍲 **10 MINS** ✗ **SERVES 2**

PER SERVING:
296 KCAL /49G CARBS

2 medium bananas
2 tbsp cornflour
¼ tsp ground cinnamon
¼ tsp grated nutmeg
1 medium egg, beaten
50g panko breadcrumbs
low-calorie cooking spray
1 tbsp Biscoff spread

Next time you fancy something sweet, grab the jar of Biscoff from the cupboard and treat yourself to these 20-minute nibbles! You'll need to slice up a couple of perfectly ripe bananas for this recipe, ready to coat in our cinnamon and nutmeg-infused panko breadcrumbs. Air-fry each bite until irresistibly crunchy, then get ready to drizzle over the melted Biscoff spread – or use it to dip if you prefer!

Weekly Indulgence

Peel and slice the bananas into bite-size slices about 2cm (¾in) thick.

Add the cornflour to a plate with the cinnamon and nutmeg and stir to combine. Add the beaten egg to a bowl and the panko breadcrumbs to a plate.

Take a banana slice and coat it in the cornflour mixture, covering all sides. Then dip it into the egg and finally into the panko. Place on a plate and coat the rest of the banana slices.

Place the coated banana slices into your air fryer basket and spray with a little low-calorie cooking spray. You may need to do this in batches, depending on the size of your air fryer. Air-fry at 180°C for 10 minutes, turning halfway through.

While the banana bites cook, place the Biscoff spread in a small bowl or cup and microwave for 20–30 seconds until just melted, and stir until smooth. You can also do this by placing the small bowl or cup containing the Biscoff spread in a larger bowl containing a little boiling water, and stir until just melted and smooth.

Once the banana bites are cooked, drizzle over the Biscoff spread or serve as a dipping sauce alongside. These are best served warm.

TIPS:

Slice the bananas when you are ready to make the bites, if you do this too far in advance, they may go brown.

This recipe is best using just ripe bananas that aren't too spotty. If your bananas are too soft, this may make them lose their shape when cooked.

SWEET TREATS

VEGGIE

FREEZE ME

BATCH COOK

GLUTEN FREE

USE GF FLOUR AND BAKING POWDER

WHITE CHOCOLATE *and* BLUEBERRY MUFFINS

🕐 **10 MINS**   🍲 **12 MINS**   ✕ **MAKES 12**

PER MUFFIN:
122 KCAL /18G CARBS

SPECIAL EQUIPMENT:
12 small silicone muffin cases (or fairy cake cases)

200g self-raising flour
1 tsp baking powder
3 tbsp granulated sweetener
50g reduced-fat spread
1 medium egg
125g fat-free natural yoghurt
100ml skimmed milk
50g white chocolate chips
100g fresh blueberries

These fluffy, berry-licious muffins will have you coming back for seconds (or thirds!). We've folded an ultra-sweet combination of white chocolate chips and tangy blueberries into our low-fat sponge, and kept things delightfully moist by beating the egg with fat-free yoghurt, reduced-fat spread and skimmed milk. Luckily, one batch of this speedy recipe makes 12 muffins, so there should be plenty to go around – plus leftovers that you can keep in an airtight container to sweeten up your week. They're perfect as a grab-and-go breakfast or cuppa-time snack!

Everyday Light

Sift the flour and baking powder together into a mixing bowl. Stir in the sweetener.

Put the spread in a small bowl and pop in the microwave for a few seconds to melt. You can also do this by placing the small bowl in a larger bowl containing a little boiling water, and stir until melted.

In a separate jug, beat the egg, yoghurt, milk and melted spread together.

Working quickly, make a well in the flour and pour in the wet ingredients. Add the white chocolate chips and blueberries and fold everything together with a spatula, until just combined.

Spoon into the silicone muffin or fairy cake cases. Place into the air fryer basket and air-fry at 160°C for 12 minutes, until risen and golden. To check if they are cooked, a skewer inserted into the centre of the muffin should come out clean. You may have to cook these in batches, depending on the size of your air fryer.

You can freeze these, once cold, in airtight freezerproof containers. Defrost and eat cold, or warm through in the microwave for a few seconds.

TIP:

Use white granulated sweetener that has the same weight, texture and sweetness as sugar.

SWEET SAMOSAS

⏲ **30 MINS**   🍲 **8 MINS**   ✕ **MAKES 8**

PER SAMOSA:
91 KCAL /15G CARBS

SPECIAL EQUIPMENT:
2 clean damp tea towels, pastry brush

2 sheets of filo pastry
2 tsp plain flour
2 tsp cold water
16 Rolos
low-calorie cooking spray
1 tsp icing sugar

The beauty of a samosa is that it can be filled with just about anything! To make these Sweet Samosas, we've opened a pack of Rolos and bundled a few inside thin, crisp filo pastry. As they air-fry, the Rolos melt into a gooey, chocolatey caramel filling, while the filo turns crunchy and golden. Give them a little dusting of icing sugar for extra pizazz, and serve them hot or cold (they're especially delicious straight out of the air fryer). The only question is, who gets the last one?

Everyday Light

Cut each filo sheet, from top to bottom, into 4 equal-sized strips. Place on a board and cover with a clean, dampened tea towel to prevent it drying out.

Mix the flour and water together to form a paste. This will be used to 'glue' your samosas.

To assemble the samosas, take one strip of pastry and brush the edges with the flour and water mix. Place 2 Rolos in the top centre of the strip. Fold one corner diagonally over the Rolos and press the edges together to seal. Repeat this folding until you reach the end of the filo strip and have a triangular-shaped parcel.

Place the finished samosa under the dampened tea towel and repeat until you have 8 samosas. You can freeze them at this point, in a freezerproof container separated with layers of greaseproof paper, then cook from frozen for the time stated below, plus a few additional minutes.

Spray the samosas on both sides with low-calorie cooking spray. Carefully place in the air fryer basket, seam side down, and air-fry for 2½ minutes at 200°C. Flip and cook for a further 2½ minutes. You may need to do this in batches, depepnding on the size of your air fryer. The samosas should be golden and crisp. If not, cook for another minute or two.

Allow the samosas to rest for a minute, then arrange on a plate and dust with icing sugar. The samosas can be served hot or cold and will stay crisp for 1–2 days if stored in an airtight container.

For freezing and reheating guidelines see page 17.

SWEET TREATS

PAVLOVAS

🕐 **20 MINS**   🍲 **45 MINS**   ✕ **SERVES 8**

PER SERVING:
116 KCAL / 18G CARBS

SPECIAL EQUIPMENT:
Electric whisk, piping bag and nozzle

3 egg whites
75g caster sugar
50g icing sugar
1 tsp cornflour
1 tsp white wine vinegar
1 tsp vanilla extract
60g mascarpone cheese
60g fat-free Greek-style
  yoghurt
200g frozen mixed berries,
  defrosted (juice saved)

These chewy in the middle, fruit-topped pavlovas are an absolute delight to whip up in an air fryer. There are no full-fat creams in our recipe; instead, we've rustled up a blend of fat-free Greek-style yoghurt and mascarpone cheese to reduce the calories, but without losing the all-important luxuriously silky centre. Pipe 8 meringues into shape, pop them in your air fryer basket and wait for the beep – 45 minutes later, you'll have a whole batch of gorgeous, impressive little nests ready to fill and decorate with juicy berries.

Everyday Light

First, prepare some baking parchment for piping the meringue mix onto. Cut it to the size of the air fryer basket. Draw 8 circles approximately 8cm (3in) in diameter and set aside for later.

Place the egg whites into a very clean mixing bowl. Make sure there is no egg yolk in the bowl with the egg whites. Start to whisk, using an electric hand whisk, until the egg whites form soft peaks. Add the caster sugar, 1 tablespoon at a time, and whisk until fully mixed in. Then sift in the icing sugar a little at a time and whisk in. The egg whites should be stiff and glossy and, when you feel the meringue mixture between your fingers, you should not be able to feel any grittiness (the sugar should be dissolved). If it is gritty, continue to whisk for another minute.

Mix the cornflour, vinegar and vanilla together in a small bowl. Pour into the meringue mixture and whisk until combined. Spoon the mixture into a piping bag fitted with a plain or star nozzle.

Carefully place the baking parchment in the air fryer basket, ink/pencil side down. You should be able to see the guidelines through the parchment.

TIP:

The meringues should feel crisp and dry and you should be able to lift them off the baking parchment easily. If they stick, you need to cook them for another 5–10 minutes.

Continued...

Pipe one layer of meringue mixture into the first circle to make a base. Make sure you stay just inside the circle, as the meringue will expand during cooking. Pipe another 3 layers on the edge of the base to make a nest. Repeat until you have 8 nests.

Place in the air fryer and air-fry for 45 minutes at 120°C. The meringue should be crisp on the outside with a soft chewy centre. If it isn't quite cooked, air-fry for another few minutes. Remove the basket from the air fryer and allow to cool for 5 minutes, then carefully remove the parchment from the air fryer basket and place each meringue nest onto a wire rack.

Mix the mascarpone and Greek-style yoghurt in a bowl until fully combined. Leave in the fridge until ready to assemble.

When the meringue nests are completely cool, fill the centre with the mascarpone mixture and spoon over the defrosted berries and their juice. Serve.

TIP:

The meringues can be made approximately 1 or 2 days in advance and stored in an airtight container. It's best to add the toppings only when ready to serve.

VEGGIE

FREEZE ME

BATCH COOK

LOW CARB

DAIRY FREE

GLUTEN FREE
USE GF SELF-RAISING FLOUR

ORANGE *and* LEMON CAKE

🕐 **10 MINS**   🍲 **25 MINS**   ✕ **SERVES 10**

PER SERVING:
88 KCAL /10G CARBS

SPECIAL EQUIPMENT:
25.5 x 13.5cm (10 x 5in) loaf tin, loaf tin baking liners, electric whisk, pastry brush

3 tbsp granulated sweetener
zest and juice of 1 large lemon
zest and juice of 1 large orange
5 medium eggs, separated
50g self-raising flour

TO ACCOMPANY *(optional)*
1 small sliced orange, pith removed (+10 kcal per slice)
50g Fat-free Greek-style yoghurt (+ 27 kcal)

It's hard to believe that you only need five ingredients to make this scrumptious sponge cake (and with an air fryer at your fingertips, it's ready in less than half an hour, too!). To get started, squeeze the juicy goodness from a large fresh lemon and a large fresh orange, and keep hold of their zest. When your loaf is risen and almost ready, you'll baste the outside with an extra layer of fruit juice, to guarantee every mouthful packs a citrus-infused punch. Delightfully fluffy and tart, it pairs like a dream with a cuppa, for only 88 calories per slice!

Everyday Light ─────────────────

Place a baking tin liner in a loaf tin.

In a mixing bowl, add 2½ tablespoons of the granulated sweetener with the lemon and orange zest. Pour in half of the juice from both the lemon and orange. Add the egg yolks and flour, then mix together.

In a separate very clean bowl, whisk the egg whites using an electric whisk until they form stiff peaks. This will take 8–9 minutes. Fold the egg whites into the flour and egg yolk mixture, until they are mixed evenly. Take care not to over-mix.

Pour the mixture into the lined loaf tin. Place in the air fryer and air-fry at 180°C for 20 minutes until golden brown, or until a skewer inserted into the centre of the cake comes out clean.

While the cake is in the air fryer, mix the remaining lemon and orange juice with the remaining ½ tablespoon of granulated sweetener.

Once the cake is cooked through, use a pastry brush to lightly coat the top of the cake with the juice and sweetener mixture.

Turn the air fryer down to 100°C and cook for a further 5 minutes.

Use a tea towel or oven glove to carefully remove the tin from the air fryer. Leave to cool in the tin for a few minutes then transfer to a wire rack. Once cool, slice into 10 evenly sized slices and serve. You can freeze the cake once cooled: place in a freezerproof container and freeze. Defrost in the fridge overnight before serving.

TIPS:

Use white granulated sweetener that has the same weight, texture and sweetness as sugar.

Do not open the air fryer while the cake is cooking as this will cause the cake to dip in the middle.

SWEET TREATS

VEGGIE

FREEZE ME

BATCH COOK

GLUTEN FREE

USE GF
PLAIN FLOUR AND
BAKING POWDER

FREEZER COOKIES

🕐 **10 MINS + 1 HOUR FREEZING**   🍲 **7 MINS**   ✕ **MAKES 15**

PER COOKIE:
153 KCAL / 24G CARBS

130g reduced-fat spread, at
    room temperature
180g granulated sweetener
220g plain flour
½ tsp baking powder
½ tsp bicarbonate of soda
1 tsp vanilla bean paste
1 medium egg
30g chocolate chips

These Freezer Cookies are the life hack you never knew you needed! Simply slice as many cookies as you want from the homemade roll of frozen dough, and air-fry to your liking (the longer you bake them, the crispier they'll be!). It only takes 10 minutes to make the cookie dough mixture; we've kept things classic by swirling in chocolate chips, but there's nothing to stop you adding frozen berries if you prefer a fruitier biscuit with your cuppa.

Everyday Light ——————————————————

Place the reduced-fat spread and granulated sweetener into a bowl and mix together until it has a creamy consistency.

In a separate bowl, mix together the plain flour, baking powder, bicarbonate of soda, vanilla bean paste and egg. Add the spread and sweetener mixture to the flour mixture and add the chocolate chips. Mix this together until it forms a dough-like consistency.

Spoon the mixture into the centre of a sheet of non-stick baking paper. Take the nearest side of paper and fold over the dough so it is fully covered. Use your hands to gently roll the dough into a cylinder approx. 5 x 30cm (2 x 12in).

Use the baking paper to wrap the dough mixture and place in the freezer for a minimum of 1 hour.

When you are ready to air-fry the cookies, remove the cookie dough from the freezer and cut into 15 slices.

Line your air fryer tray with a sheet of non-stick baking paper, tucking the edges under so they can't flap around. Carefully place the cookies on the baking paper, making sure there is space around each cookie. You may need to bake them in batches, depending on the size of your air fryer.

If you like your cookies soft and gooey, air-fry at 170°C for 5 minutes. If you prefer your cookies firm and more like a biscuit, air-fry for 7 minutes.

With a pair of tongs, carefully remove the cookies from the air fryer, re-shaping them if you want perfect circles, and leave to cool.

TIPS:

Use white granulated sweetener that has the same weight, texture and sweetness as sugar.

Use a silicone mat in the air fryer.

SWEET TREATS

VEGGIE

FREEZE ME

BATCH COOK

GLUTEN FREE

USE GF FLOUR AND BAKING POWDER

CREAM TEA SCONES

🕐 **20 MINS**   🍲 **5 MINS**   ✕ **MAKES 16**

PER SCONE:
94 KCAL /18G CARBS

SPECIAL EQUIPMENT:
5cm (2in) plain round pastry cutter or a glass

250g self-raising flour, plus extra for dusting
2 tsp baking powder
25g reduced-fat spread
15g granulated sweetener
15g caster sugar
1 medium egg, beaten
120ml skimmed milk
2 tbsp milk, for brushing

FOR THE TOPPING
100g fat-free, thick Greek-style yoghurt
1 tsp icing sugar
100g reduced-sugar strawberry jam
8 small strawberries, stalks left on and halved

TIPS:

Make sure to measure the baking powder accurately and use 2 level teaspoons, not rounded or heaped teaspoonfuls.

Use white granulated sweetener that has the same weight, texture and sweetness as sugar.

Scones cut out with a plain cutter or glass tend to rise better than those cut out with a fluted cutter.

Fancy a spot of afternoon tea? These Cream Tea Scones look and taste just as luxurious as cafe-bought versions, for a fraction of the calories you'd expect. To keep our scones slimming-friendly, we've used reduced-sugar ingredients to recreate the famous layers of scrumptious jam and cream. They only need 5 minutes in the air fryer before they're golden and ready to decorate with a juicy strawberry slice – that's your cue to pop the kettle on!

Everyday Light ———————————————

Sift the flour and baking powder into a medium mixing bowl. Add the reduced-fat spread and rub in with your fingertips until the mixture resembles fine breadcrumbs. Stir the sweetener and sugar into the mixture until well combined.

Place the beaten egg in a jug and add the milk. Mix with a fork until completely combined.

Add the egg and milk mixture to the flour mixture and mix in using a round-bladed knife to form a very soft dough.

Scrape the dough out onto a floured surface and knead lightly for a few seconds to make a smooth, soft dough. The dough will be very soft so you will need to flour your hands.

Gently roll out the dough using a floured rolling pin to a thickness of 1cm (½in). Use a 5cm (2in) plain round cutter or upturned glass to cut out 16 scones. Flouring the rim of your cutter or glass will make it easier to cut out the scones. You will need to gather up and re-roll the scraps to make all 16 scones.

Line your air fryer basket with a sheet of non-stick baking paper. Place the scones on the paper, leaving space between each. Brush the tops only with the milk and air-fry at 200°C for 5 minutes until risen and golden. You may need to cook these in batches, depending on the size of your air fryer.

Carefully remove from the air fryer and transfer to a wire rack to cool completely. While scones taste their best freshly baked, you can freeze them. Place them in a freezerproof box and freeze them as soon as they've cooled. Defrost in the fridge overnight and then allow to come to room temperature before serving.

While the scones are cooling, make the creamy filling. Place the yoghurt and icing sugar in a small bowl and mix well.

Cut the cooled scones in half using a serrated knife. Spread a small amount of jam in a thin layer on each scone half. Spoon a small amount of sweetened yoghurt on top of the jam and top each with half a strawberry. Serve alone or as part of a selection of teatime treats.

Store any leftover scones in an airtight container for up to 3 days in the fridge. Remove and allow to come to room temperature before serving.

APPLE UPSIDE-DOWN TARTS

⏰ **10 MINS** 🍲 **10 MINS** ✕ **MAKES 8**

VEGGIE

FREEZE ME

BATCH COOK

DAIRY FREE
USE DF PUFF PASTRY

GLUTEN FREE
USE GF PASTRY

PER TART:
129 KCAL /17G CARBS

SPECIAL EQUIPMENT:
Pastry brush

1 Bramley apple
200g ready-rolled light puff pastry sheet, cut into 8cm (3in) squares
2 tbsp reduced-sugar marmalade
1 medium egg, beaten
1 tsp icing sugar

If you have a spare 20 minutes and five simple ingredients, you could be tucking into one of these sweet, juicy Apple Upside-down Tarts with your next cuppa. An easy-peasy combination of flaky puff pastry, sticky marmalade and crisp apple slices, these are ideal for rustling up when you're expecting guests. They look and taste impressive, despite being incredibly quick to make and low in calories too! Try bundling one up to take in your packed lunch – it'll make an afternoon tea break at your desk so much sweeter.

Everyday Light

Peel, core and cut the apple into slices about the thickness of a £1 coin.

Line the air fryer basket with non-stick baking paper and lay the apple slices into sections about the size of your 8cm (3in) squares of puff pastry. You may need to do this in batches, depending on the size of your air fryer.

Add the marmalade to a small bowl and stir to loosen. Using a pastry brush, coat one side of each puff pastry square. Place it marmalade-side down onto the apple and press the edges down onto the non-stick baking paper. You can use your fingertips or press down with a fork.

Brush the top of the pastry with the beaten egg and air-fry at 180°C for 10 minutes. After 8 minutes, gently turn the tarts over so that the apple is now on the top. Brush the apple with the remaining marmalade and cook for a further 2 minutes.

Leave to cool slightly before removing from the air fryer. Dust with icing sugar and serve. To freeze, let them cool completely and freeze in a single layer in an airtight, freezerproof container. For standard defrosting and reheating guidelines see page 17.

USE DF
BUTTER
ALTERNATIVE

USE GF
FLOUR

CHURRO SWIRLS

🕐 **5 MINS**   🍲 **30 MINS + 5 MINS RESTING**   ✗ **MAKES 6**

PER SWIRL:
189 KCAL /30G CARBS

SPECIAL EQUIPMENT:
Piping bag with star-shaped nozzle

1½ tbsp brown granulated
  sweetener
55g unsalted reduced-fat butter
125ml water
¼ tsp salt
90g plain flour
½ tsp vanilla extract
1 egg

FOR THE COATING
1 tbsp granulated sweetener
1 tsp ground cinnamon

Some churro recipes can be challenging to rustle up, but these air-fried swirls are ready in just a few simple steps with a short list of budget-friendly ingredients. You'll want to make sure you're using granulated sweeteners with the same weight and texture as sugar, so that your churro batter (and the cinnamon coating they'll be dipped in) is just as sweet as restaurant versions. When the batter ingredients combine and turn glossy, it's time to get piping! We've used a star-shaped nozzle to create golden-brown churro spirals that look and taste gorgeous.

Everyday Light

In a small saucepan, combine the sweetener, butter, water and salt. Heat slowly over a medium heat until the butter has melted, then bring to the boil and take off the heat. Tip in the flour and beat until the mixture forms a ball and comes away from the sides of the pan. Add the vanilla extract and egg. The mixture will look like it has separated at first, but carry on mixing and it will come back together and turn glossy.

Line your air fryer basket with non-stick baking paper. Transfer half the mixture into a piping bag fitted with a star-shaped nozzle. It is easiest to pipe with half the mixture first, then you can refill the bag with the rest of the mixture.

Pipe the mixture onto the baking paper in an outward direction. As you are piping, leave 1cm (½in) around each coil. Each churro should be approximately 3 coils wide. Pipe another churro onto the baking paper, making sure it does not touch the first churro.

The mixture should make 6 churros, but you will need to air-fry in batches. Air-fry the churros at 160°C for 30 minutes until they are crispy and golden brown.

While the churros are cooking, mix the sweetener and ground cinnamon in a large bowl.

When the churros are cooked, using tongs, carefully remove them from the air fryer. Dip each churro into the sweetener mix, coating them on all sides. Place on a wire rack and leave to cool for 5 minutes, then serve warm!

TIP:

Use granulated sweetener that has the same weight, texture and sweetness as sugar.

SWEET TREATS

CHOCOLATE BROWNIE LOAF

⏱ **5 MINS**   🍲 **10 MINS**   ✕ **SERVES 16**

PER SERVING:
64 KCAL / 6.6G CARBS

SPECIAL EQUIPMENT:
Two 18 x 9cm (7 x 4in)
loaf tins, or one square
18cm (7in) cake tin

50g reduced-fat spread
100g self-raising flour
4 tbsp granulated sweetener
1 tsp baking powder
4 medium eggs
2 tbsp cocoa powder
4 tsp Sweet Freedom Choc Shot
25g dark chocolate chips

Nothing brings more joy than a warm, squidgy slice of Chocolate Brownie Loaf! This air fryer recipe cooks in just 10 minutes, with only 5 minutes of prep and a short list of basic baking ingredients. To make our treats gooey and chocolatey for fewer calories, we've said goodbye to calorie-laden ingredients and hello to slimming-friendly alternatives. Topped with a layer of chocolate chips, you won't believe this heavenly recipe is as light as 64 calories per square!

Everyday Light ───────────────

Line your loaf tins or cake tin with non-stick baking paper.

Place the reduced-fat spread, flour, granulated sweetener, baking powder, eggs, cocoa and Choc Shot into a large mixing bowl and mix thoroughly.

Pour into the lined loaf tins or baking tin and sprinkle over the dark chocolate chips. Place into the air fryer and air-fry at 170°C for 10 minutes.

To check that your brownie loaf is cooked through, insert a skewer into the centre. If the skewer comes out clean, your brownie loaf is cooked. If not, continue cooking for another 2 minutes and check again.

Once cooked, turn out onto a wire rack and remove the baking paper. Cut into 8 slices per loaf, or 16 squares if you've used one tin.

Serve warm or cold!

If you want to freeze, once cool, place in a freezerproof container and freeze. For standard defrosting guidelines see page 17.

TIP:

Use white granulated sweetener that has the same weight, texture and sweetness as sugar.

FAN FAVOURITE

'Easy to make and so chocolatey and delicious.'
Sarah-Jane Rich

SWEET TREATS

NUTRITIONAL INFO

BREAKFAST	ENERGY KJ/KCAL	FAT (G)	SATURATED FAT (G)	CARBS (G)	SUGAR (G)	FIBRE (G)	PROTEIN (G)
BREAKFAST BAKE	1153/275	11	3.5	12	4.2	4.1	30
LOADED HASH BROWN	1674/397	9.2	2.1	56	7.4	7.1	19
BACON AND CHEESE FRITTATA	1365/327	18	6.3	4.3	2.4	0.5	36
SAUSAGE AND EGG MUFFIN	1733/413	17	6.8	27	12	5.2	37
BANANA AND RASPBERRY FRENCH TOAST	1531/366	7.5	2.5	51	26	2.7	13
CINNAMON BREAKFAST BUNS	596/141	1.8	0.4	26	2.9	1.5	4.7
PEACH MELBA BAKED OATS	728/173	5	1.1	23	4.7	2.7	9.6

FAKEAWAYS	ENERGY KJ/KCAL	FAT (G)	SATURATED FAT (G)	CARBS (G)	SUGAR (G)	FIBRE (G)	PROTEIN (G)
CHEESY GARLIC NAANZONE	1367/324	5.7	2.6	49	3.6	2.7	17
CHAR-SIU-STYLE PORK TENDERLOIN	1210/288	11	3.9	9.7	8.8	0	37
BBQ PULLED CHICKEN	786/186	2.1	0.5	9.1	7.8	1.5	31
ZINGER BURGERS	1500/356	8.3	1.7	29	2.5	4	39
TEX-MEX STYLE CHICKEN	1776/421	12	2.5	17	4.7	1.6	62
SWEET POTATO KATSU	1386/328	4.1	0.9	60	21	9	9
STICKY TERIYAKI AUBERGINE	290/69	0.8	0.2	11	10	3.3	2.1
SHISH KEBAB	1109/263	5.5	2.2	15	10	3.9	36
SALT AND PEPPER CHIPS	1568/370	0.8	0.2	77	7.4	10	8.8
PIZZA TURKEY BURGERS	1572/372	6.3	2.4	42	9.2	4.3	33
MADRAS MEATBALLS	1244/296	9.2	3.2	16	12	5.8	34
LOADED CHEESEBURGER FRIES	1963/466	12	6.4	45	8.4	5.5	40
KUNG PAO PORK	1269/301	6.7	2.1	33	15	3.9	24

FAKEAWAYS	ENERGY KJ/KCAL	FAT (G)	SATURATED FAT (G)	CARBS (G)	SUGAR (G)	FIBRE (G)	PROTEIN (G)
GOCHUJANG CHICKEN NUGGETS	985/233	3.2	0.8	22	12	0.5	29
FISH AND CHIPS FISHCAKES	782/185	4.4	1	17	3.6	2.3	18
FETA-STUFFED FALAFELS	723/172	4.9	2.1	15	4.8	4.3	14
CURRY PUFFS	1082/258	10	4.5	33	3.7	3.4	6.6
CRISPY CHILLI BEEF	1175/279	7.2	2.6	19	10	2.6	32
CHICKEN TIKKA MASALA	1048/248	3.5	1.6	16	13	3.4	35
CHICKEN SOUVLAKI & TZATZIKI	933/220	2.4	0.6	5.2	4.1	1.6	43
CHICKEN IN ORANGE	1138/269	3.3	0.7	27	15	0.9	31
CHICKEN AND SWEETCORN PIZZA CALZONE	2010/479	17	7.7	31	8	5.7	48
CHICKEN AND PINEAPPLE SKEWERS	892/211	1.6	0.4	16	16	1.6	31

BAKES & ROASTS	ENERGY KJ/KCAL	FAT (G)	SATURATED FAT (G)	CARBS (G)	SUGAR (G)	FIBRE (G)	PROTEIN (G)
CRISPY LEMON AND PARMESAN CHICKEN	868/206	5.9	2.3	6.5	2.1	1.9	30
CREAMY PESTO SALMON	1434/345	25	5.8	3.6	1.1	0.6	26
WHOLE CHICKEN	1163/278	17	4.8	1.6	0.7	1.6	31
SAUSAGE TRAYBAKE	1511/359	7	2	53	29	9	17
SAUSAGE PASTA BAKE	2081/494	13	6.1	56	16	7.6	33
COSY PIGS IN THE HOLE	1727/411	14	4.4	31	6.1	2.8	38
CHICKEN KYIV PASTA BAKE	1714/406	8.6	4.3	48	6.1	5	33
CHEESY POTATO GRATIN	993/236	5.6	3.4	32	6.4	2.7	13
SALMON FISHCAKES	1054/250	4.1	0.9	26	3	5	24
CHEESE AND BACON FILO TARTS	698/167	7.9	3.1	8	1.4	0	16
BBQ MEATLOAF	999/237	6.2	2.8	14	8.3	2.5	30

BAKES & ROASTS	ENERGY KJ/KCAL	FAT (G)	SATURATED FAT (G)	CARBS (G)	SUGAR (G)	FIBRE (G)	PROTEIN (G)
ROASTED PARMESAN SPROUTS	415/99	4.2	1.9	5.6	3.9	5.2	7.2
ROAST POTATOES	1334/315	0.7	0.2	66	3.4	7.6	7.1
MAPLE-GLAZED GAMMON	1096/262	4.3	1.1	14	14	0.8	41
MAPLE-GLAZED CARROTS AND PARSNIPS	398/95	1.3	0.3	16	9.9	6.4	1.9
KOFTE MEATBALL BAKE	1071/254	6.3	2.7	7.2	5	3.1	41
LASAGNE	1042/248	9.1	5	11	9.3	3.8	29
HUNTER'S CHICKEN	1343/331	8.2	3.6	11	8.6	1.7	51
FLUFFY JACKET POTATOES WITH SPICY TUNA	1274/301	1.2	0.3	51	7.9	5.8	18
FLUFFY JACKET POTATOES	908/214	0.7	0.1	45	2.3	5	47

LIGHT BITES	ENERGY KJ/KCAL	FAT (G)	SATURATED FAT (G)	CARBS (G)	SUGAR (G)	FIBRE (G)	PROTEIN (G)
AIR FRYER CHICKPEAS - GARLIC AND HERB	1060/252	3.3	0.5	34	1.1	13	15
AIR FRYER CHICKPEAS - MOROCCAN SPICED	1072/255	3.4	0.5	34	1.1	13	15
AIR FRYER CHICKPEAS - SMOKY PAPRIKA	1066/253	3.5	0.5	34	1.2	13	15
AIR FRYER CHICKPEAS - SWEET CINNAMON	1089/259	3.3	0.5	36	1	13	15
VIKING CROQUETTES	537/128	4.9	1.2	16	0.9	1.5	4
SWEET POTATO AND FETA PARCELS	476/113	2.5	1.3	17	1.9	1.3	5.5
SMOKY BACON SCOTCH EGGS	1076/257	11	3.1	11	2.5	2.1	27
CHEESE, ONION AND SWEETCORN STUFFED PEPPERS	647/155	6.8	3.8	14	12	4.1	7.4
SAUSAGE ROLLS	716/170	5.2	1.9	12	1.6	1.8	18
POTATO DOGS	1386/329	5.8	1.9	41	4.7	5.7	25
PIZZA SWIRLS	210/50	2.4	1.2	4.9	0.5	0.5	1.9
GOUDA AND CRANBERRY TOASTIE	1866/448	29	6	32	5.4	5.3	12

LIGHT BITES	ENERGY KJ/KCAL	FAT (G)	SATURATED FAT (G)	CARBS (G)	SUGAR (G)	FIBRE (G)	PROTEIN (G)
CHEESY ROASTED VEGETABLE SOUP	555/132	3.1	1.5	18	14	4.9	4.7
CHEESE AND ONION BAKES	923/220	9.1	4.8	20	2.8	1.4	14
CHEESE AND CHIVE SCONES	396/94	2.3	1.2	13	0.5	0.7	4.5
BROCAULI BITES	451/107	2.8	1	13	2.3	2.8	7.2
BLOOMING ONION WITH DIPPING SAUCE	1026/245	9.9	1.8	28	13	4.9	8.7
ALOO BORA	184/44	0.5	0	7.6	0.7	1.1	1.5

SWEET TREATS	ENERGY KJ/KCAL	FAT (G)	SATURATED FAT (G)	CARBS (G)	SUGAR (G)	FIBRE (G)	PROTEIN (G)
CHERRY BAKEWELL SLICES	382/91	3.2	0.5	13	3.7	0.6	2.2
BISCOFF BANANA BITES	1250/296	7.3	2	49	21	2.1	6.9
WHITE CHOCOLATE AND BLUEBERRY MUFFINS	511/122	4.5	1.5	18	4.3	0.8	3.5
SWEET SAMOSAS	381/91	2.7	1.2	15	6.8	0.6	1.4
PAVLOVAS	489/116	3.4	2.2	18	18	0.7	2.6
ORANGE AND LEMON CAKE	368/88	2.7	0.8	10	2.4	1.1	4.4
FREEZER COOKIES	644/153	5.7	2.3	24	1.6	0.5	1.7
CREAM TEA SCONES	396/94	1.2	0.3	18	5.2	0.6	2.8
APPLE UPSIDE-DOWN TARTS	540/129	5.3	2.3	17	4.7	1.4	3.2
CHURRO SWIRLS	796/189	6.5	1.5	30	0	0.7	2.6
CHOCOLATE BROWNIE LOAF	268/64	3.1	1	6.6	1.5	0	2.5

INDEX

Page numbers in **bold** refer to illustrations

ACKNOWLEDGEMENTS

We owe many thank yous to many people who have worked so hard to bring this book together. Out of all the books so far, this one has probably been the most challenging. Without these people, this book would not exist. We deeply appreciate you all and can't thank you enough for the time and hard work put into making this book something we are so very proud of.

We want to say a huge thank you firstly to all of our followers who have been asking for this book for SO long. Thank you to those who continue to make our recipes and let us know what you want next. We're so proud that Pinch of Nom has helped and continues to help so many people.

Thank you to our publisher Lizzy Gray. To Katy Denny, Bríd Enright, Jodie Lancet-Grant, Annie Rose, Amy Winchester, Sarah Badhan and the rest of the team at Bluebird for helping us create this book and for continuing to believe in Pinch of Nom throughout our journey. Major thanks also to our agent Clare Hulton for your unwavering support, guidance and teaching us the power of the word 'no'.

To Mike English for the amazing photos and to Kate Wesson and Max Robinson for making our food look so, so good. Thanks also to Kristine Jakobsson for all your assistance. Big thanks go out to Emma Wells and Nikki Dupin at Nic & Lou for making this book so beautiful!

We also want to thank our friends and family who have made this book possible. A very big thank you to Dr Hannah Cowan, Helen Child Villiers, Katie McKenna, Emma & Nicola Brooks. Your support has meant the absolute world.

Special thanks go to Katie Mitchell and Rosie Sparrow for the endless hours you've put into this and for working so hard to get things right, especially given the very tight deadlines!

A huge thank you to our wonderful team of recipe developers who work tirelessly to help us bring these recipes to life; Lisa Allinson, Sharon Fitzpatrick and Holly Levell. To Cate Meadows and Matthew Maney for going the extra mile.

Massive thanks also go to Sophie Fryer, Hannah Cutting, Nick Nicolaou, Ellie Drinkwater and Laura Valentine for your writing and marketing support. To Jacob Lathbury for your creative visuals. Just genius!

Additional thanks to Jessica Molyneux, Rubi Bourne & Vince Bourne for supporting us and the business - we are so proud to work alongside you all.

To our wonderful moderators and online support team; thank you for all your hard work keeping the peace and for all your support.

Furry thanks to Mildred, Wanda, Ginger Cat and Freda & the fishies for the daily moments of joy.

And finally; huge thanks go to Paul Allinson for your support and advice. And to Cath Allinson who will never be forgotten #YNWA

First published 2024 by Bluebird
an imprint of Pan Macmillan
The Smithson, 6 Briset Street, London EC1M 5NR
EU representative: Macmillan Publishers Ireland Ltd, 1st Floor,
The Liffey Trust Centre, 117–126 Sheriff Street Upper,
Dublin 1, D01 YC43

Associated companies throughout the world
www.panmacmillan.com

ISBN 978-1-0350-5456-5

1 3 5 7 9 8 6 4 2
A CIP catalogue record for this book is available from the British Library.
Printed and bound in Italy

Art Direction Nikki Dupin and Emma Wells, Nic&Lou
Design Emma Wells, Nic&Lou
Illustration Shutterstock / Emma Wells
Photography Mike English
Food Styling Kate Wesson, Kristine Jakobssen
Prop Styling Max Robinson

Visit www.panmacmillan.com to read more about all our books
and to buy them. You will also find features, author interviews and
news of any author events, and you can sign up for e-newsletters
so that you're always first to hear about our new releases.